# COTTON KNITS for all seasons

# COTTON KNITS for all seasons

## 25 projects for babies, children and adults

## Debbie Bliss

Trafalgar Square Publishing

*For Raewyn, Hans, Max and Sam.*

First published in the United States of America in 2002 by
Trafalgar Square Publishing, North Pomfret, Vermont 05053

10 9 8 7 6 5 4 3 2 1

Library of Congress Catalog Card Number: 2001094247

ISBN 1 57076 218 X

Edited by Kate Haxell
Photography by Craig Fordham
Styling by Sammi Bell
Designed by Sara Kidd
Illustrations by Stephen Dew and Kate Simunek

# contents

# INTRODUCTION

*Cotton Knits For All Seasons* has given me a great opportunity to design knits that show the versatility of cotton. There are 25 designs for adults and children, ranging from pretty summer cardigans to hooded tops and a Nordic-inspired blanket, jacket and hat for a winter baby.

Cotton is cool in the summer and warm in the winter, making it a great all-year-round yarn. The pure cotton double knitting yarn knits up quickly and smoothly to create colorful motif knits, and clearly shows the stitch detail in the textured knits. I have also used my wool/cotton mix – which is an ideal combination as it gives a yarn with the elasticity of wool and the crispness of cotton – in simple baby designs and in a shaped, body-skimming cardigan for an adult, while my cotton/silk mix yarn adds glamor to an aran style.

There are designs here for a range of knitting skills, but the emphasis is on simple, stylish knits. However, for less experienced knitters who want to expand their skills there are step-by-step diagrams for colorwork and cables.

Debbie Bliss

# EMBROIDERED dress

A simple, sleeveless dress with mock pleats is embellished with a swag of embroidery on the yoke. This design is not only perfect as a summer dress, but also works well as a winter pinafore, worn over a long-sleeved top.

**Materials**

7(8:9) 50g balls of Debbie Bliss cotton double knitting. Pair each of US 3 (3¼mm) and US 6 (4mm) knitting needles. Small amounts of yarn in five colors for embroidery (see page 122).

**Measurements**

| To fit ages | 1 | 2 | 3 | years. |
|---|---|---|---|---|
| *Actual measurements* | | | | |
| Chest | 20 | 22 | 24 | in |
| | 51 | 56 | 61 | cm |
| Length to shoulder | 17½ | 19¼ | 21 | in |
| | 44 | 49 | 53 | cm |

**Gauge**

20 sts and 28 rows to 4in/10cm square over st st using US 6 (4mm) needles.

**Abbreviations**

See page 127.

**BACK**

With US 6 (4mm) needles cast on 122(134:146) sts.

**1st rib row** K4, p5, ★ k7, p5; rep from ★ to last 5 sts, k5.

**2nd rib row** P5, k5, ★ p7, k5; rep from ★ to last 4 sts, p4.

These 2 rows set the rib patt.

Work a further 8(18:28) rows.

**Dec row (right side)** K4, p2, p2tog, p1, ★ k7, p2, p2tog, p1; rep from ★ to last 5 sts, k5.

Work 9 rows rib as set.

**Dec row (right side)** K4, p4,★ k3, skpo, k2, p4; rep from ★ to last 5 sts, k5.

Work 9 rows rib as set.

**Dec row (right side)** K4, p1, p2tog, p1,★ k6, p1, p2tog, p1; rep from ★ to last 5 sts, k5.

Work 9 rows rib as set.

**Dec row (right side)** K4, p3, ★ k2, skpo, k2, p3; rep from ★ to last 5 sts, k2, skpo, k1.

Work 9 rows rib as set.

**Dec row (right side)** K4, p1, p2tog, ★ k5, p1, p2tog; rep from ★ to last 4 sts, k4.

Work 9 rows rib as set.

**Dec row (right side)** K1, skpo, k1, p2, ★ k1, skpo, k2, p2; rep from ★ to last 4 sts, k4.

Work 9 rows rib as set.

**Dec row (right side)** K3, ★ p2tog, k4; rep from ★ to end. 53(58:63) sts.

Cont in rib as set until back measures 11(12½:14¼)in/28(32:36)cm from cast on edge, ending with a wrong side row.

Beg with a k row work 4(6:8) rows st st.

### Shape armholes

**Next row** Bind off 3 sts at the beg of the next 2 rows.

Dec one st at each end of the next 2 rows then every foll alt row until 39(44:49) sts rem. Work straight until back measures 17(18¾:20½)in/43(48:52)cm from cast on edge, ending with a wrong side row.

### Shape back neck

**Next row** K8(10:11), turn and work on these sts for first side of neck.

Work 1 row.

**Next row** K6(8:9), k2 tog.

Work 1 row.

Bind off rem 7(9:10) sts.

With right side facing, slip center 23(24:27) sts on a holder, rejoin yarn to rem sts and k to end.

Work 1 row.

**Next row** Skpo, k to end.

Work 1 row.

Bind off rem 7(8:9) sts.

### FRONT

Work as given for Back until 14(16:18) rows less have been worked than Back to shoulder shaping, ending with a wrong side row.

### Shape neck

**Next row** K12(14:15), turn and work on these sts for first side of neck.

Work 1 row.

**Next row** K10(12:13), k2tog.

Work 1 row.

Rep last 2 rows until 8(10:11) sts rem.

Cont straight until front measures same as Back to shoulder shaping, ending with a wrong side row.

Bind off.

With right side facing, slip center 15(16:19) sts on a holder, rejoin yarn to rem sts and work as given for left side reversing shapings.

### NECKBAND

Join left shoulder seam.

With US 3 (3¼mm) needles and right side facing, pick up and k14(15:16) sts down left front neck, k15(16:19) sts from front neck holder, pick up and k14(15:16) sts up right front neck, 4 sts down right back neck, k23(24:27) sts from back neck holder, pick up and k4 sts up left back neck. 74(78:86) sts.

**1st row** K2, ★ p2, k2; rep from ★ to end.
**2nd row** P2, ★ k2, p2; rep from ★ to end.
Rep the last 2 rows once more.
Bind off in rib.

### ARMBANDS (BOTH ALIKE)

Join right shoulder seam.

With US 3 (3¼mm) needles and right side facing, pick up and k62(70:78) sts around armhole edge.
Work 4 rows in rib as given for Neckband.
Bind off in rib.

### FINISH

Using satin stitch, lazy daisy and French knots, work embroidery on front yoke as shown in diagram above and on page 122.
Join side seams.

# BABY BOBBLE jacket

This textured cardigan is knitted in a wool/cotton mix in a soft, dusky pink. The bobble and cable pattern is echoed in the neat garter stitch borders with bobble detailing.

## Materials

5(5:6) 50g balls of Debbie Bliss wool/cotton. Pair each of US 2 (2¾mm) and US 3 (3¼mm) knitting needles. Cable needle. 5 buttons.

## Measurements

| To fit ages | 3-6 | 6-9 | 9-12 | months. |
|---|---|---|---|---|
| *Actual measurements* | | | | |
| Chest | 23½ | 24¾ | 26 | in |
| | 60 | 63 | 66 | cm |
| Length to shoulder | 9½ | 10¼ | 11 | in |
| | 24 | 26 | 28 | cm |
| Sleeve length | 5½ | 6¼ | 7 | in |
| | 14 | 16 | 10 | cm |

## Gauge

25 sts and 34 rows to 4in/10cm square over st st using US 3 (3¼mm) needles.

## Abbreviations

**Tw4Rb** – slip next st onto cable needle and leave at back, k1b, p1, k1b, then p1 from cable needle.
**Tw4Lb** – slip next 3 sts onto cable needle and leave at front, p1, then k1b, p1, k1b, from cable needle.
**Mb** – work k1, p1, k1, p1, k1, into next st, turn, p5, turn, k5, pass 2nd, 3rd, 4th and 5th st over first and off the needle.
**C4F** – slip next 2 sts onto cable needle and leave at front, k2, then k2, from cable needle.
See also pages 118 and 127.

## PATT PANEL

(worked over 23(25:25) sts)
**1st row (right side)** P7(8:8), Tw4Rb, k1b, Tw4Lb, p7(8:8).
**2nd row** K7(8:8), p1, [k1, p1] 4 times, k7(8:8).
**3rd row** P6(7:7), Tw4Rb, k1, k1b, k1, Tw4Lb, p6(7:7).
**4th row** K6(7:7), p1, k1, p1, [k2, p1] twice, k1, p1, k6(7:7).
**5th row** P5(6:6), Tw4Rb, k2, k1b, k2, Tw4Lb, p5(6:6).
**6th row** K5(6:6), p1, k1, p2, k2, p1, k2, p2, k1, p1, k5(6:6).
**7th row** P4(5:5), Tw4Rb, k1b, [k2, k1b] twice, Tw4Lb, p4(5:5).
**8th row** K4(5:5), p1, [k1, p1] twice, [k2, p1] twice, [k1, p1] twice, k4(5:5).
**9th row** P3(4:4), Tw4Rb, k1, k1b, [k2, k1b] twice, k1, Tw4Lb, p3(4:4).
**10th row** K3(4:4), p1, k1, p1, [k2, p1] 4 times, k1, p1, k3(4:4).
**11th row** P2(3:3), Tw4Rb, k2, [k1b, k2] 3 times, Tw4Lb, p2(3:3).
**12th row** K2(3:3), p1, k1, p1, k3, p1, [k2, p1] twice, k3, p1, k1, p1, k2(3:3).
**13th row** P2(3:3), k1b, p1, k1b, k3, Mb, [k2, Mb] twice, k3, k1b, p1, k1b, p2(3:3).
**14th row** K2(3:3), p1, k1, p1, k3, p1b, [k2, p1b] twice, k3, p1, k1, p1, k2(3:3).
**15th row** P2(3:3), k1b, p1, k1b, p3, k1b, p1, [k1b] 3 times, p1, k1b, p3, k1b, p1, k1b, p2(3:3).
**16th row** K8(9:9), p1, k1, p3, k1, p1, k8(9:9).
These 16 rows form the patt and are repeated throughout.

## BACK

With US 2 (2¾mm) needles cast on
87(91:97) sts.

K 3 rows to form garter st hem.

**Next row** K4(3:3) ★ Mb, k5; rep from ★ to
last 5(4:4) sts, Mb, k4(3:3).

K 3 rows, inc one st at end of last row on 1st
and 2nd sizes only. 88(92:97) sts.

Change to US 3 (3¼mm) needles.

**1st row** K15(15:17), work across 1st row of
patt panel, k12(12:13), work across 1st row of
patt panel, k15(15:17).

**2nd row** K3(3:4), p4, k4(4:5), p4, work across
2nd row of patt panel, p4, k4(4:5), p4, work
across 2nd row of patt panel, p4, k4(4:5), p4,
k3(3:4).

**3rd row** K3(3:4), C4F, k4(4:5), C4F, work
across 3rd row of patt panel, C4F, k4(4:5),
C4F, work across 3rd row of patt panel, C4F,
k4(4:5), C4F, k3(3:4).

**4th row** K3(3:4), p4, k4(4:5), p4, work across
4th row of patt panel, p4, k4(4:5), p4, work
across 4th row of patt panel, p4, k4(4:5), p4,
k3(3:4).

These 4 rows **set** the position for patt panels
and form garter st and cable panels.

Cont in patt until back measures
9½(10¼:11)in/24(26:28)cm from cast on edge,
ending with a wrong side row.

### Shape shoulders

Bind off 14(14:15) sts at beg of next 2 rows
and 14(15:16) sts on foll 2 rows.

Bind off rem 32(34:35) sts.

## LEFT FRONT

With US 2 (2¾mm) needles cast on
46(48:50) sts.

K 3 rows.

**Next row** K4(3:3) ★ Mb, k5; rep from ★ to
last 6(9:5) sts, Mb, k5(8:4).

K 3 rows.

Change to US 3 (3¼mm) needles.

**1st row** K15(15:17), work across 1st row of
patt panel, k8.

**2nd row** K4, p4, work across 2nd row of patt
panel, p4, k4(4:5), p4, k3(3:4).

**3rd row** K3(3:4), C4F, k4(4:5), C4F, work
across 3rd row of patt panel, C4F, k4.

**4th row** K4, p4, work across 4th row of patt

panel, p4, k4(4:5), p4, k3(3:4).

These 4 rows **set** the position for patt panels and form garter
st and cable panels.

Cont in patt until front measures 8(8¾:9½)in/20(22:24)cm
from cast on edge, ending with a wrong side row.

### Shape neck

**Next row** Patt to last 8 sts, leave these sts on a safety-pin,
turn and work on rem sts.

Dec one st at neck edge on every row until 28(29:31)
sts rem.

Work straight until front measures same as Back to shoulder
shaping, ending at side edge.

### Shape shoulder

Bind off 14(14:15) sts at beg of next row.

Work 1 row.

Bind off rem 14(15:16) sts.

Mark positions for buttons: the first 1¼in/3cm from cast on
edge, the fifth ½in/1cm from neck edge, the rem three
spaced evenly between.

## RIGHT FRONT

Work buttonholes to match markers as folls:

**Buttonhole row (right side)** K1, k2 tog, yf, k1, patt to end.

With US 2 (2¾mm) needles cast on 46(48:50) sts.

K 3 rows.

**Next row** K5(8:4) ★ Mb, k5; rep from ★ to last 5(4:4) sts,
Mb, k4(3:3).

K 3 rows.

Change to US 3 (3¼mm) needles.

**1st row** K8, work across 1st row of patt panel, k15(15:17).

**2nd row** K3(3:4), p4, k4(4:5), p4, work across 2nd row of
patt panel, p4, k4.

**3rd row** K4, C4F, work across 3rd row of patt panel, C4F,
k4(4:5), C4F, k3(3:4).

**4th row** K3(3:4), p4, k4(4:5), p4, work across 4th row of patt
panel, p4, k4.

These 4 rows **set** the position for patt panels and form garter
st and cable panels.

Cont in patt until front measures 8(8¾:9½)in/20(22:24)cm
from cast on edge, ending with a right side row.

### Shape neck

**Next row** Patt 8 sts, leave these sts on a safety-pin, patt
to end.

Dec one st at neck edge on every row until 28(29:31)
sts rem.

Work straight until front measures same as Back to shoulder
shaping, ending at side edge.

**Shape shoulder**

Bind off 14(14:15) sts at beg of next row.

Work 1 row.

Bind off rem 14(15:16) sts.

**SLEEVES**

With US 2 (2¾mm) needles cast on 41(45:49) sts.

K 3 rows.

**Next row** K5(4:3) ★ Mb, k5; rep from ★ to last 6(5:4) sts, Mb, k5(4:3).

K 3 rows.

Change to US 3 (3¼mm) needles.

**1st row** K9(10:12), work across 1st row of patt panel, k9(10:12).

**2nd row** P1(2:3), k4(4:5), p4, work across 2nd row of patt panel, p4, k4(4:5), p1(2:3).

**3rd row** K1(2:3), k4(4:5), C4F, work across 3rd row of patt panel, C4F, k4(4:5), k1(2:3).

**4th row** P1(2:3), k4(4:5), p4, work across 4th row of patt panel, p4, k4(4:5), p1(2:3).

These 4 rows **set** the position for patt panels and form garter st and cable panels.

Cont in patt as set **at the same time** inc one st at each end of the next and every foll 4th row until there are 57(63:71) sts, working first 3(2:1) sts into cable panel and the rem sts in reverse st st.

Cont straight until sleeve measures 5½(6¼:7)in/14(16:18)cm from cast on edge, ending with a wrong side row.

Bind off.

**COLLAR**

Join shoulder seams.

With right side facing using US 2 (2¾mm) needles, slip 8 sts from safety-pin onto a needle, pick up and k12 sts up right front, 29 sts from back neck, pick up and k12 sts down left side of front neck, k8 from safety-pin. 69 sts.

**Next row** K to end.

Beg with a p row cont in st st with 4 sts in garter st at each end.

**Next 2 rows** Work to last 15 sts, turn.

**Next 2 rows** Work to last 10 sts, turn.

Work to end.

**Next row** Bind off 2 sts, k to end.

**Next row** Bind off 2 sts, k next 3 sts, p to last 4 sts, k4.

**Next row** K to end.

**Next row** K4, p to last 4 sts, k4.

Rep the last 2 rows once more.

**Next row** K2, Mb, k to last 3 sts, Mb, k2.

**Next row** K4, p to last 4 sts, k4.

Rep the last 6 rows once more.

K 4 rows.

**Next row** K2, ★ Mb, k5; rep from ★ to last 3 sts, Mb, k2.

K 2 rows.

Bind off.

**FINISH**

Sew on sleeves. Join side and sleeve seams.

Sew on buttons.

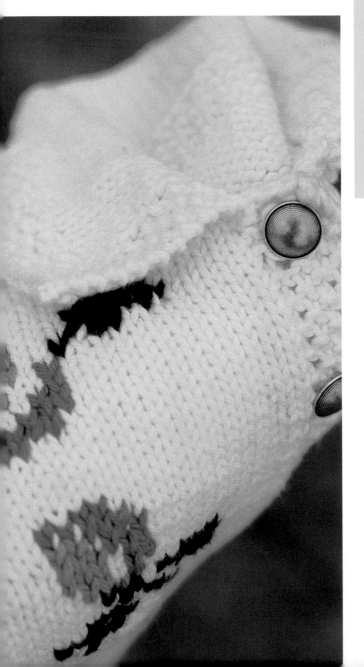

# FLORAL jacket

This is a great jacket for the summer. It can look pretty and dressed-up or sporty and casual. The design would look equally effective worked in lighter, toning shades against a dark background, such as pinks on navy blue.

## Materials

6(7) 50g balls of Debbie Bliss cotton double knitting in White (M). One ball each of Navy Blue, Dark Blue and Mid Blue. Pair each of US 3 (3¼mm) and US 6 (4mm) knitting needles. 7(8) buttons.

## Measurements

| To fit ages | 2-3 | 3-4 | years. |
|---|---|---|---|
| *Actual measurements* | | | |
| Chest | 30¾ | 33 | in |
| | 78 | 84 | cm |
| Length to shoulder | 12¼ | 13¾ | in |
| | 31 | 35 | cm |
| Sleeve length | 8¼ | 9½ | in |
| | 21 | 24 | cm |

## Gauge

20 sts and 28 rows to 4in/10cm square over st st using US 6 (4mm) needles.

## Abbreviations

See page 127.

## Note

When working motifs, use separate balls of yarn for each area of color and twist yarns together on wrong side to avoid holes (see page 116).

## BACK

With US 3 (3¼mm) needles and M cast on 72(78) sts and work seed st hem.
**1st row** ★ K1, p1; rep from ★ to end.
**2nd row** ★ P1, k1; rep from ★ to end.
Rep the last 2 rows 3 times more.
Change to US 6 (4mm) needles.
Beg with a k row, work 0(2) rows st st.
**1st row** K5(7)M, reading chart from right to left, k across 1st row of Chart, k16(18)M, reading chart from left to right, k across 1st row of Chart, k5(7)M.
**2nd row** P5(7)M, reading chart from right to left, p across 2nd row of Chart, p16(18)M, reading chart from left to right, p across 2nd row of Chart, p5(7)M.
**3rd row** K5(7)M, reading chart from right to left, k across 3rd row of Chart, k16(18)M, reading chart from left to right, k across 3rd row of Chart, k5(7)M.
**4th row** P5(7)M, reading chart from right to

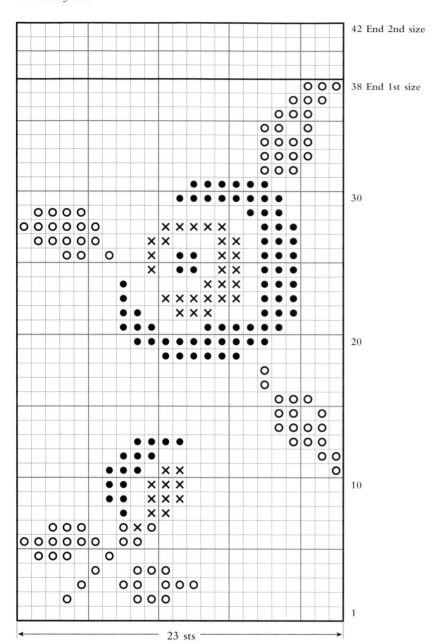

42 End 2nd size

38 End 1st size

30

20

10

1

|← 23 sts →|

**Key**

☐ Main

◉ Navy Blue

☒ Mid Blue

● Dark Blue

left, p across 4th row of Chart, p16(18)M, reading chart from left to right, p across 4th row of Chart, p5(7)M.

These 4 rows set the 38(42) row patt.

Cont in patt **at the same time** inc one st at each end of the next every foll 8th row until there are 80(86) sts.

Work straight until 40(46) rows have been worked, ending with a wrong side row.

**Shape armholes**

Bind off 4 sts at beg of next 2 rows.

Cont straight until 76(86) rows have been worked from top of seed st hem.

Cont in M only.

Work 2(4) rows in st st, then work 6 rows in seed st.

**Shape shoulders**

Bind off 12(13) sts at beg of next 4 rows.

Leave rem 24(26) sts on a holder.

**LEFT FRONT**

With US 3 (3¼mm) needles and M cast on 38(40) sts.

Work 8 rows seed st as given for Back, inc 0(1) st at center of last row. 38(41) sts.

Change to US 6 (4mm) needles.

*2nd size only*

**Next row** K to last 5 sts, seed st 5.

**Next row** Seed st 5, p to end.

**Both sizes**

**1st row** K5(7)M, reading chart from right to left, k across 1st row of Chart, k5(6)M, seed st 5.

**2nd row** Seed st 5, p5(6), reading chart from left to right, p across 2nd row of Chart, p5(7)M.

**3rd row** K5(7)M, reading chart from right to left, k across 3rd row of Chart, k5(6)M, seed st 5.

**4th row** Seed st 5, p5(6)M, reading chart from left to right, p across 4th row of Chart, p5(7)M.

These 4 rows set the 38(42) row patt.

Cont in patt to match Back, **at the same time** inc one st at side edge of the next and every foll 8th row until there are 42(45) sts.

Work straight until 40(46) rows have been worked, ending with a wrong side row.

**Shape armhole**

Bind off 4 sts at beg of next row.

Cont straight until 70(80) rows have been worked, ending with a wrong side row.

**Shape neck**

**Next row** Patt to last 5 sts, turn, leave rem sts on a safety-pin.

Bind off 3 sts at beg of next row and 2(3) sts at beg of foll alt row.

Dec one st at neck edge on every row until 24(26) sts rem.

Work 6 rows seed st.

**Shape shoulder**

Bind off 12(13) sts at beg of next row.

Patt 1 row.

Bind off rem 12(13) sts.

Mark positions for buttons on left front, the first to come on the 3rd row from cast on edge, the last to come 2 rows below neck shaping, and rem 3(4) spaced evenly between.

**RIGHT FRONT**

With US 3 (3¼mm) needles and M cast on
38(40) sts.

Work 2 rows seed st as given for Back.

**Buttonhole row** Seed st 2, work 2 tog, yon,
seed st 1, patt to end.

Work 5 rows seed st.

Change to US 6 (4mm) needles.

*2nd size only*

**Next row** Seed st 5, k to end.

**Next row** P to last 5 sts, seed st 5.

*Both sizes*

**1st row** Seed st 5, k5(6)M, reading chart from left to right, k
across 1st row of Chart, k5(7)M.

**2nd row** P5(7)M, reading chart from right to left, p across

2nd row of Chart, p5(6)M, seed st 5.
**3rd row** Seed st 5, k5(6)M, reading chart from left to right, k across 3rd row of Chart, k5(7)M.
**4th row** P5(7)M, reading chart from right to left, p across 4th row of Chart, p5(6)M, seed st 5.
These 4 rows set the 38(42) row patt.
Complete to match Left Front, reversing shapings and making buttonholes as before to match markers.

### SLEEVES

With US 3 (3¼mm) needles and M cast on 38(42) sts.
Work 11 rows seed st as given for Back.
**Inc row** Seed st 6(2), * m1, seed st 4; rep from * to end. 46(52) sts.
Change to US 6 (4mm) needles
Beg with a k row, work 0(2) rows st st.
**1st row** Reading chart from right to left, k across last 19(21) sts of 1st row of Chart, k8(10)M, reading chart from left to right, k across first 19(21) sts of 1st row of Chart.
**2nd row** Reading chart from right to left, p across last 19(21) sts of 2nd row of Chart, p8(10)M, reading chart from left to right, p across first 19(21) sts of 2nd row of Chart.
These 2 rows set the 38(42) row patt.
Work in patt from Chart **at the same time** inc and work into st st one st at each end of the next and every foll 5th row until there are 64(72) sts.
Cont straight until 56(64) rows have been worked from top of cuff.
Bind off.

### COLLAR

Join shoulder seams.
With right side facing using US 6 (4mm) needles and M slip sts from safety-pin on right front onto a needle, pick up and k21(22) sts to right shoulder, k24(26) from back neck holder, pick up and k 21(22) sts to beg of neck shaping, work across sts on safety pin. 76(80) sts.
**Next row** Seed st 8, k to last 8 sts, seed st 8.

#### Shape Collar

**1st row** Bind off 4 sts, seed st next 3 sts, p46(49) sts, turn.
**2nd row** K32(34) sts, turn.
**3rd row** P36(38) sts, turn.
**4th row** K40(42) sts, turn.
Cont in this way for a further 2 turning rows, taking an extra 4 sts, as before, on each row, turn, work to end.
**Next row** Bind off 4 sts, seed st next 3 sts, k to last 4 sts, seed st 4 sts.
**Next row** Seed st 4, p to last 4 sts, seed st 4.
**Next row** Seed st 4, m1, k to last 4 sts, m1, seed st 4.

**Next row** Seed st 4, p to last 4 sts, seed st 4.
**Next row** Seed st 4, k to last 4 sts, seed st 4.
Rep the last 4 rows twice more.
Seed st 5 rows across all sts.
Bind off in patt.

### STRAPS (MAKE 2)

With US 6 (4mm) needles and M cast on 7 sts.
Work 3¼in/8cm in seed st.
**Buttonhole row** Seed st 3, yf, work 2 tog, seed st 2.
Work 2 rows.
Cont in seed st, dec one st at each end of the next 2 rows.
**Next row** Sl 1, k2 tog, psso and fasten off.

### FINISH

Sew on sleeves, sewing last 6 rows to sts bind off at underarm. Join side and sleeve seams. Place straps on top of front welts and sew cast on edges to side seams. Sew on buttons.

# CABLE hooded jacket

With a zip front and hood, this neat cabled jacket can take the place of the sweatshirt in your essentials wardrobe. The casual top works all the year round, whether for sporty outerwear or relaxing in the house.

**Materials**

20(21:23:24) 50g balls of Debbie Bliss cotton double knitting. Pair each of US 3 (3¼mm) and US 6 (4mm) knitting needles. Cable needle. 18(18:20:20)in/45(45:50:50)cm open-ended zip.

**Measurements**

| To fit | | 32 | 34 | 36 | 38 | in |
|---|---|---|---|---|---|---|
| | | 81 | 86 | 91 | 96 | cm |
| *Actual measurements* | | | | | | |
| Bust | | 34½ | 38 | 41 | 44 | in |
| | | 88 | 96 | 104 | 112 | cm |
| Length to shoulder | | 20½ | 20¾ | 21½ | 22 | in |
| | | 52 | 53 | 55 | 56 | cm |
| Sleeve length | | 17 | 17 | 17¼ | 17¼ | in |
| | | 43 | 43 | 44 | 44 | cm |

**Gauge**

20 sts and 28 rows to 4in/10cm square over st st using US 6 (4mm) needles.
Patt panel over 18 sts measures 2½in/6cm.

**Abbreviations**

**C3F** – slip next 2 sts onto cable needle and leave at front, k1, then k2 from cable needle.
**C3B** – slip next st onto cable needle and leave at back, k2, then k1 from cable needle.
**T3F** – slip next 2 sts onto cable needle and leave at front, p1, then k2 from cable needle.
**T3B** – slip next st onto cable needle and leave at back, k2, then p1 from cable needle.
**C4F** – slip next 2 sts onto cable needle and leave at front, k2, then k2 from cable needle.
**C4B** – slip next 2 sts onto cable needle and leave at back, k2, then k2 from cable needle.
See also pages 118 and 127.

**PATT PANEL**

(worked over 18 sts)
**1st row (right side)** P7, C4B, p7.
**2nd row** K7, p4, k7.
**3rd row** P6, C3B, C3F, p6.
**4th row** K6, p6, k6.
**5th row** P5, C3B, k2, C3F, p5.
**6th row** K5, p8, k5.
**7th row** P4, T3B, C4B, T3F, p4.
**8th row** K4, p2, k1, p4, k1, p2, k4.
**9th row** P3, T3B, p1, k4, p1, T3F, p3.
**10th row** K3, p2, k2, p4, k2, p2, k3.
**11th row** P2, T3B, p2, C4B, p2, T3F, p2.
**12th row** K2, p2, k3, p4, k3, p2, k2.

**13th row** P1, T3B, p3, k4, p3, T3F, p1.
**14th row** K1, p2, k4, p4, k4, p2, k1.
**15th row** P1, k2, p4, C4B, p4, k2, p1.
**16th row** As 14th row.
**17th row** P1, T3F, p3, k4, p3, T3B, p1.
**18th row** As 12th row.
**19th row** P2, T3F, p2, C4B, p2, T3B p2.
**20th row** As 10th row.
**21st row** P3, T3F, p1, k4, p1, T3B, p3.

**22nd row** As 8th row.
**23rd row** P4, T3F, C4B, T3B, p4.
**24th row** As 6th row.
**25th row** P5, T3F, k2, T3B, p5.
**26th row** As 4th row.
**27th row** P6, T3F, T3B, p6.
**28th row** K7, p4, k7.
These 28 rows form the patt and are repeated throughout.

## BACK

With US 3 (3¼mm) needles cast on 124(132:140:148) sts.

**1st row** [K2, p2] 1(2:3:4) times, ★ k4, [p2, k2] twice, p2; rep from ★ to last 8(12:16:20) sts, k4, [p2, k2] 1(2:3:4) times.

**2nd row** [P2, k2] 1(2:3:4) times, ★ p4, [k2, p2] twice, k2; rep from ★ to last 8(12:16:20) sts, p4, [k2, p2] 1(2:3:4) times.

**3rd row** [K2, p2] 1(2:3:4) times, ★ C4F, [p2, k2] twice, p2, C4B, [p2, k2] twice, p2; rep from ★ to last 8(12:16:20) sts, C4F, [p2, k2] 1(2:3:4) times.

**4th row** [P2, k2] 1(2:3:4) times, ★ p4, [k2, p2] twice, k2; rep from ★ to last 8(12:16:20) sts, p4, [k2, p2] 1(2:3:4) times.

Rep the last 4 rows for 3in/8cm, ending with a 1st row.

**Inc row** [P2, k2] 1(2:3:4) times, ★ p4, [k2, p2] twice, k2, m1p, p4, m1p, [k2, p2] twice, k2; rep from ★ to last 8(12:16:20) sts, k4, [p2, k2] 1(2:3:4) times. 132(140:148:156) sts.

Change to US 6 (4mm) needles.

**1st row** [K2, p2] 1(2:3:4) times, ★ C4F, p2, k2, work across 1st row of patt panel, k2, p2; rep from ★ to last 8(12:16:20) sts, C4F, [p2, k2] 1(2:3:4) times.

**2nd row** [P2, k2] 1(2:3:4) times, ★ p4, k2, p2, work across 2nd row of patt panel, p2, k2; rep from ★ to last 8(12:16:20) sts, p4, [k2, p2] 1(2:3:4) times.

**3rd row** [K2, p2] 1(2:3:4) times, ★ k4, p2, k2, work across 3rd row of patt panel, k2, p2; rep from ★ to last 8(12:16:20) sts, k4, [p2, k2] 1(2:3:4) times.

**4th row** [P2, k2] 1(2:3:4) times, ★ p4, k2, p2, work across 4th row of patt panel, p2, k2; rep from ★ to last 8(12:16:20) sts, p4, [k2, p2] 1(2:3:4) times.

These 4 rows set the position for patt panels and form cable panels.

Cont in patt until back measures 12¼(12½:12½:13)in/31(32:32:33)cm from cast on edge, ending with wrong side row.

### Shape armholes

Bind off 6 sts at beg of next 2 rows.

Dec one st at each end of next and 4(6:8:10) foll alt rows. 102(106:110:114) sts.

Cont in patt until back measures 20½(20¾:21½:22)in/52(53:55:56)cm from cast on edge, ending with a right side row.

**Next row** Patt to end, dec 10 sts evenly over cable sections. 92(96:100:104) sts.

### Shape shoulders

Bind off 25(27:29:31) sts at beg of next 2 rows.

Bind off rem 42 sts.

## LEFT FRONT

With US 3 (3¼mm) needles cast on 61(65:69:73) sts.

**1st row** [K2, p2] 1(2:3:4) times, ★ k4, [p2, k2] twice, p2; rep from ★ to last 15 sts, k4, p2, k2, p2, k5.

**2nd row** K3, [p2, k2] twice, ★ p4, [k2, p2] twice, k2; rep from ★ to last 8(12:16:20) sts, p4, [k2, p2] 1(2:3:4) times.

**3rd row** [K2, p2] 1(2:3:4) times, C4F, [p2, k2] twice, p2, C4B, [p2, k2] twice, p2, C4F, [p2, k2] twice, p2, C4B, p2, k2, p2, k5.

**4th row** K3, [p2, k2] twice, ★ p4, [k2, p2] twice, k2; rep from ★ to last 8(12:16:20) sts, p4, [k2, p2] 1(2:3:4) times.

Rep the last 4 rows for 3in/8cm, ending with a 1st row.

**Inc row** K3, [p2, k2] twice, m1p, p4, m1p, [k2, p2] twice, k2, p4, [k2, p2] twice, k2, m1p, p4, m1p, [k2, p2] twice, k2, p4, [k2, p2] 1(2:3:4) times. 65(69:73:77) sts.

Change to US 6 (4mm) needles.

**1st row** [K2, p2] 0(1:2:3) times, ★ k2, p2, C4F, p2, k2, work across 1st row of patt panel; rep from ★ once more, k5.

**2nd row** K3, p2, ★work across 2nd row of patt panel, p2, k2, p4, k2, p2; rep from ★ once more, [k2, p2] 0(1:2:3) times.

**3rd row** [K2, p2] 0(1:2:3) times, ★ k2, p2, k4, p2, k2, work across 3rd row of patt panel; rep from ★ once more, k5.

**4th row** K3, p2, ★ work across 4th row of patt panel, p2, k2, p4, k2, p2; rep from ★ once more, [k2, p2] 0(1:2:3) times.

These 4 rows set the position for patt panels and form cable panels.

Cont in patt until front measures 12¼(12½:12½:13)in/31(32:32:33)cm from cast on edge, ending with wrong side row.

### Shape armhole

Bind off 6 sts at beg of next row.

Patt 1 row.

Dec one st at armhole edge of next and 4(6:8:10) foll alt rows. 54(56:58:60) sts.

Cont in patt until front measures 19(19¼:20:20½)in/48(49:51:52)cm from cast on edge, ending with a wrong side row.

p2, C4F, [p2, k2] twice, p2, C4B, [p2, k2] twice, p2, C4F, [p2, k2] 1(2:3:4) times.

**4th row** [P2, k2] 1(2:3:4) times, ★ p4, [k2, p2] twice, k2; rep from ★ to last 15 sts, p4, [k2, p2] twice, k3.

Rep the last 4 rows for 3in/8cm, ending with a 1st row.

**Inc row** [P2, k2] 1(2:3:4) times, p4, [k2, p2] twice, k2, m1p, p4, m1p, [k2, p2] twice, k2, p4, [k2, p2] twice, k2, m1p, p4, m1p, [k2, p2] twice, k3. 65(69:73:77) sts.

Change to US 6 (4mm) needles.

**1st row** K5, ★ work across 1st row of patt panel, k2, p2, C4F, p2, k2; rep from ★ once more, [p2. k2] 0(1:2:3) times.

**2nd row** [P2, k2] 0(1:2:3) times, ★ p2, k2, p4, k2, p2, work across 2nd row of patt panel; rep from ★ once more, p2, k3.

**3rd row** K5, ★ work across 3rd row of patt panel, k2, p2, k4, p2, k2; rep from ★ once more, [p2. k2] 0(1:2:3) times.

**4th row** [P2, k2] 0(1:2:3) times, ★ p2, k2, p4, k2, p2, work across 4th row of patt panel; rep from ★ once more, p2, k3.

These 4 rows set the position for patt panels and form cable panels.

Cont in patt until front measures 12¼(12½:12½:13)in/31(32:32:33)cm from cast on edge, ending with right side row.

## Shape armhole

Bind off 6 sts at beg of next row.

Dec one st at armhole edge of next and 4(6:8:10) foll alt rows. 54(56:58:60) sts.

Cont in patt until front measures 19(19¼:20:20½)in/ 48(49:51:52)cm from cast on edge, ending with a wrong side row.

## Shape neck

**Next row** Patt 23 sts, leave these sts on a holder, patt to end.

Cont straight until front measures same as Back to shoulder shaping, ending with a right side row.

**Next row** Patt to end, dec 6 sts evenly over cable sections. 25(27:29:31) sts.

## Shape shoulder

Bind off.

## Shape neck

**Next row** Patt to last 23 sts, leave these sts on a holder, turn and work on rem sts for front neck.

Cont straight until front measures same as Back to shoulder shaping, ending with a wrong side row.

**Next row** Patt to end, dec 6 sts evenly over cable sections. 25(27:29:31) sts.

## Shape shoulder

Bind off.

## RIGHT FRONT

With US 3 (3¼mm) needles cast on 61(65:69:73) sts.

**1st row** K5, p2, k2, p2, ★ k4, [p2, k2] twice, p2; rep from ★ to last 8(12:16:20) sts, k4, [p2, k2] 1(2:3:4) times.

**2nd row** [P2, k2] 1(2:3:4) times, ★ p4, [k2, p2] twice, k2; rep from ★ to last 15 sts, p4, [k2, p2] twice, k3.

**3rd row** K5, p2, k2, p2, C4B, [p2, k2] twice,

**SLEEVES**
Using US 3 (3¼mm) needles cast on 58 sts.
**1st rib row** K2, ★ p2, k2; rep from ★ to end.
**2nd rib row** P2, ★ k2, p2; rep from ★ to end.
Rep the last 2 rows for 2½in/6cm, ending with a first row.
**Inc row** P2, ★ m1, p2, m1, [k2, p2] twice, k2, m1, inc in each of next 2 sts, m1, [k2, p2] twice, k2; rep from ★ once more, m1, p2, m1, k2, p2. 72 sts.
**1st row** K2, p2, ★ C4F, p2, k2, work across 1st row of patt panel, k2, p2; rep from ★ to last 8 sts, C4F, p2, k2.
**2nd row** P2, k2, ★ p4, k2, p2, work across 2nd row of patt panel, p2, k2; rep from ★ to last 8 sts, p4, k2, p2.
**3rd row** K2, p2, ★ k4, p2, k2, work across 3rd row of patt panel, k2, p2; rep from ★ to last 8 sts, k4, p2, k2.
**4th row** P2, k2, ★ p4, k2, p2, work across 4th row of patt panel, p2, k2; rep from ★ to last 8 sts, p4, k2, p2.
These 4 rows set the position for patt panels and form cable panels.
Cont in patt as set **at the same time** inc one st at each end of the next and every foll 10th(10th:8th:8th) row until there are 92(92:98:98) sts, working first 6 inc sts in p2, k2, p2 rib, the next 4 sts in cable patt, the rem sts in reverse st st.
Cont straight until sleeve measures 17(17:17¼:17¼)in/43(43:44:44)cm from cast on edge, ending with a wrong side row.

**Shape sleeve top**
Bind off 6 sts at beg of next 2 rows.
Dec one st at each end of next and every foll alt row until 56 sts rem, ending with a wrong side row.
Dec one st at each end of every row until 32 sts rem.
Bind off 3 sts at beg of next 4 rows.
Bind off rem 20 sts.

**HOOD**
Join shoulder seams.
With US 6 (4mm) needles, right side facing, place 23 sts from right front neck on needle, pick up and k12 sts up right side of front neck, cast on 48 sts, pick up and k 12 sts down left side of front neck, patt across sts of left front neck. 118 sts.
Keeping 3 edge sts in garter st, cont in patt until hood measures 11in/28cm, ending with a wrong side row.

**Shape top**
**Next row** Patt 59 sts, turn and work on these sts for first side of hood.
Bind off 10 sts at beg of next and 4 foll alt rows.
Work 1 row.
Bind off rem 9 sts.

With right side facing, rejoin yarn to rem sts, bind off 10 sts, patt to end.
Complete to match first side.

**FINISH**
Join top seam of hood. Sew cast on edge of hood to bound off sts at back neck. Sew on sleeves. Join side and sleeve seams. Sew in zip.

# SWEATER WITH ribbed yoke

A classic style with a textured yoke
made up of ribs and simple cable
twists, and a distinctive cross-over
collar. This is a great project for
new knitters, as most of the design
is worked in stockinette stitch.

## Materials

9(11:13) 50g balls of Debbie Bliss cotton
double knitting. Pair each of US 5 (3¾mm) and
US 6 (4mm) needles. Long circular US 5
(3¾mm) needle.

## Measurements

| To fit ages | 2-3 | 3-4 | 4-5 | years. |
|---|---|---|---|---|
| *Actual measurements* | | | | |
| Chest | 28½ | 31½ | 34½ | in |
| | 72 | 80 | 88 | cm |
| Length | 13¾ | 15¾ | 17¾ | in |
| | 35 | 40 | 45 | cm |
| Sleeve length | 8¾ | 10 | 11 | in |
| | 22 | 25 | 28 | cm |

## Gauge

20 sts and 28 rows to 4in/10cm square over st st
using US 6 (4mm) needles.

## Abbreviations

Tw2R – k into front of 2nd st, then front of 1st st and
slip both sts off the needle together.
See also page 127.

## BACK

With US 5 (3¾mm) needles cast on
74(82:90) sts.
**1st row** K2, ★ p2, k2; rep from ★ to end.
**2nd row** P2, ★ k2, p2; rep from ★ to end.
Rep the last 2 rows 4(5:6) times more.
Change to US 6 (4mm) needles.
Beg with a k row, work in st st until back
measures 18(21:24)/7(8¼:9½)in from cast on
edge, ending with a k row.
**Inc row** P5(5:4), [m1, p7(8:9) sts] 9 times, m1,
p6(5:5). 84(92:100) sts.
Cont in yoke patt.
**1st row** K3, ★ p2, Tw2R, p2, k2; rep from ★ to
last 9 sts, p2, Tw2R, p2, k3.
**2nd row** P3, ★ k2, p2; rep from ★ to last 5 sts,
k2, p3.
Rep the last 2 rows until back measures
13¾(15¾:17¾)in/35(40:45)cm from cast on
edge, ending with a wrong side row.

### Shape shoulders

Bind off 12(13:14) sts at beg of next 4 rows.
Leave the rem 36(40:44) sts on a holder.

## FRONT

Work as given for Back until front measures 11¾(13½:15)in/30(34:38)cm from cast on edge, ending with a wrong side row.

### Shape neck

**Next row** K31(34:37), turn and work on these sts for first side of neck.

Dec one st at neck edge on every row until 24(26:28) sts rem.

Cont straight until front measures the same as Back to shoulder, ending at side edge.

### Shape shoulder

Bind off 12(13:14) sts at beg of next row.
Work 1 row.

Bind off rem 12(13:14) sts.

With right side facing, slip center 22(24:26) sts onto a holder, rejoin yarn to rem sts, patt to end.

Complete to match first side.

## SLEEVES

With US 5 (3¾mm) needles cast on 42(46:50) sts.

**1st row** K2, ★ p2, k2; rep from ★ to end.

**2nd row** P2, ★ k2, p2; rep from ★ to end.

Rep the last 2 rows 4(5:6) times more, inc 2(4:4) sts evenly across last row. 44(50:54) sts.

Change to US 6 (4mm) needles.

Work in st st, inc one st at each end of the 3rd(5th:3rd) and every foll 4th row until there are 64(70:76) sts, ending with an inc row.

**Inc row** P5(5:6), [m1, p18(12:9) sts] 3(5:7) times, m1, p5(5:7). 68(76:84) sts.
Cont in yoke patt.
**1st row** K3, ★ p2, Tw2R, p2, k2; rep from ★ to last 9 sts, p2, Tw2R, p2, k3.
**2nd row** P3, ★ k2, p2; rep from ★ to last 5 sts, k2, p3.
Cont in patt **at the same time** inc and work into patt one st at each end of the next and 1(2:3) foll 4th rows.
72(82:92) sts
Cont straight until sleeve measures 8¾(10:11)in/22(25:28)cm from cast on edge, ending with a wrong side row.
Bind off.

## COLLAR

Join shoulder seams.
With right side facing, using US 5 (3¾mm) circular needle, slip 22(24:26) sts from center front neck onto needle, pick up and k21(23:25) sts up right side of front neck, k across 36(40:44) sts from back neck holder, pick up and k21(23:25)

sts down left side of front neck, turn and cast on 22(24:26) sts. 122(134:146) sts.
Work backwards and forwards in k2, p2, rib as folls:
**Next row** K2, [p2, k2] 20(22:24) times, turn.
**Next row** P2, [k2, p2] 10(11:12) times, turn.
Cont in rib as set.
**Next 2 rows** Rib to last 38(42:46) sts, turn.
**Next 2 rows** Rib to last 36(40:44) sts, turn.
**Next 2 rows** Rib to last 34(38:42) sts, turn.
Cont in this way, working 2 extra sts on every row until all sts have been worked.
Bind off loosely in rib.

## FINISH

Sew cast on edge of collar to back of center front sts. Sew on sleeves Join side and sleeve seams.

# SCARF WITH fair isle border

As it is worked mainly in seed stitch this scarf is reversible. Its simple Fair Isle border makes it a good project for those new to this style of knitting. For added decoration there are beads worked into the cast on and bound off rows.

**Materials**

Four 50g balls of Debbie Bliss cotton double knitting in Main Color (M). One ball each of Khaki, Red, Turquoise, Brown, Pink, and Yellow. Pair of US 6 (4mm) needles. 14 medium-size wooden beads.

**Measurements**

43¼in x 6in/110cm x 15cm.

**Gauge**

21 sts and 32 rows to 4in/10cm square over seed st using US 6 (4mm) needles.

**Abbreviations**

See page 127.

**Note**

Read chart from right to left on right side rows and from left to right on wrong side rows (see page 113). When working in patt, strand yarn not in use loosely across wrong side (see page 114). For border beside patt, use a separate ball of M and the intarsia method (see page 116). Knitting with beads (see page 120).

**TO MAKE**

Thread seven beads onto first ball of M. Make a slip knot and place on needle, ★bring a bead up along the yarn next to the needle, cast on 5 sts; rep from ★ 5 times more, bring a bead up along the yarn next to the needle, cast on one st. 32 sts.

**Next row** [K1, p1] 7 times, k1, p2tog, ★ k1, p1; rep from ★ to last st, k1. 31 sts.

**Next row** K1, ★ p1, k1; rep from ★ to end. This row sets the seed st.

Work 4 more rows in seed st.

★★ **Next row** Seed st 5, p21, seed st 5.

Work in patt from Chart as folls:

**1st row** Seed st 5, k next 21 sts from Chart, seed st 5.

This row sets the patt.

Working 5 edge sts in seed st and Chart in st st, work to end of Chart. Cont in M.

**Next row** Seed st 5, p21, seed st 5. ★★★

**Next row** K1, ★ p1, k1; rep from ★ to end. This row sets the seed st.

Cont in seed st until scarf measures 41¼in/105cm from cast on edge, ending with a right side row.

Work from ★★ to ★★★.

Work 6 rows seed st across all sts, inc one st at center of the last row. 32 sts.

**Bind off row** Cut the yarn approximately 3ft (1 metre) from work. Thread on seven beads. P1,★ bring bead up yarn to needle and p the next st holding bead between the two sts with thumb, bind off 5 sts purlwise; rep from ★ ending last rep bind off one st, fasten off.

| | | ● | | | | ● | | | | ● | | | 13 |
| | ● | ● | ● | | ● | | ● | | ● | ● | ● | | |
| ◣ | ◣ | ○ | ◣ | ◣ | ◣ | ○ | ◣ | ◣ | ◣ | ○ | ◣ | ◣ | |
| ◣ | ○ | ○ | ○ | ◣ | ○ | ○ | ○ | ◣ | ○ | ○ | ○ | ◣ | 10 |
| ○ | ○ | ■ | ○ | ○ | ○ | ■ | ○ | ○ | ○ | ■ | ○ | ○ | |
| ○ | ■ | ■ | ■ | ○ | ○ | ■ | ○ | ○ | ■ | ■ | ■ | ○ | |
| — | ✕ | — | ✕ | — | ✕ | — | ✕ | — | ✕ | — | ✕ | — | |
| ○ | ■ | ■ | ■ | ○ | ○ | ○ | ○ | ○ | ■ | ■ | ■ | ○ | |
| ○ | ○ | ■ | ○ | ○ | ○ | ■ | ○ | ○ | ○ | ■ | ○ | ○ | 5 |
| ◣ | ○ | ○ | ○ | ◣ | ○ | ○ | ○ | ◣ | ○ | ○ | ○ | ◣ | |
| ◣ | ◣ | ○ | ◣ | ◣ | ◣ | ○ | ◣ | ◣ | ◣ | ○ | ◣ | ◣ | |
| | ● | ● | ● | | ● | | ● | | ● | ● | ● | | |
| | | ● | | | | ● | | | | ● | | | |

**Key**

☐ Main

◣ Khaki

✕ Red

● Turquoise

■ Brown

○ Pink

— Yellow

8 stitch repeat

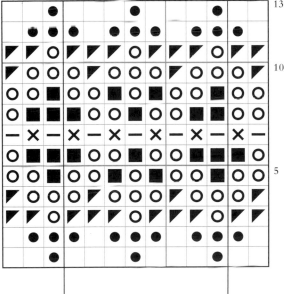

# BABY REEFER JACKET and hat

I love a classic double-breasted style. In this design it is achieved by simply picking up stitches from the fronts and working a double rib. Here I have teamed the jacket with the striped sweater on page 86.

## Materials
Jacket: 8(9:11:12) 50g balls of Debbie Bliss cotton double knitting. Pair each of US 5 (3¾mm) and US 6 (4mm) knitting needles, 6(6:8:8) buttons.
Hat: Two 50g balls of Debbie Bliss cotton double knitting. Pair of US 6 (4mm) knitting needles.

## Measurements
Jacket

| To fit ages | 6-12 | 12-18 | 18-24 | 24-36 months. |
|---|---|---|---|---|
| *Actual measurements* | | | | |
| Chest | 25¼ | 27½ | 30 | 32¼ in |
| | 64 | 70 | 76 | 82 cm |
| Length to shoulder | 11¾ | 13¾ | 15½ | 17 in |
| | 30 | 35 | 39 | 43 cm |
| Sleeve length | 7 | 8 | 9 | 10¼ in |
| (cuff turned back) | 18 | 20 | 23 | 26 cm |

Hat

| To fit ages | 6-18 | 18-36 months. |
|---|---|---|

## Gauge
20 sts and 28 rows to 4in/10cm square over st st using US 6 (4mm) needles.

## Abbreviations
See page 127.

## JACKET
### BACK
With US 5 (3¾mm) needles cast on 66(70:78:82) sts.
**1st row** K2, ★ p2, k2; rep from ★ to end.
**2nd row** P2, ★ k2, p2; rep from ★ to end
Rep the last 2 rows for 2¾in/7cm, ending with a 2nd row and inc 0(2:0:2) sts evenly across last row. 66(72:78:84) sts.
Change to US 6 (4mm) needles.
Beg with a k row cont in st st until back measures 11¾(13¾:15½:17)in/30(35:39:43)cm from cast on edge, ending with a p row.

### Shape shoulders
Bind off 11(12:13:14) sts at beg of next 2 rows and 12(13:14:14) sts at beg of foll 2 rows.
Bind off rem 20(22:24:28) sts on a spare needle.

### LEFT FRONT
With US 5 (3¾mm) needles cast on 23(23:27:27) sts.
**1st row** K2, ★ p2, k2; rep from ★ to last 5 sts, p2, k3.
**2nd row** P3, ★ k2, p2; rep from ★ to end.
Rep the last 2 rows for 2¾in/7cm, ending with a 2nd row and inc 0(2:0:1) sts evenly across last row. 23(25:27:28) sts.
Change to US 6 (4mm) needles.
Beg with a k row cont in st st until front measures 11¾(13¾:15½:17)in/30(35:39:43)cm from cast on edge, ending with a p row.

**Shape shoulder**
Bind off 11(12:13:14) sts at beg of next row.
Work 1 row.
Bind off rem 12(13:14:14) sts.

**RIGHT FRONT**
With US 5 (3¾mm) needles cast on
23(23:27:27) sts.
1st row K3, ★ p2, k2; rep from ★ to end.
2nd row P2, ★ k2, p2; rep from ★ to last 5 sts,
k2, p3.
Rep the last 2 rows for 2¾in/7cm, ending
with a 2nd row and inc 0(2:0:1) sts evenly
across last row. 23(25:27:28) sts.
Change to US 6 (4mm) needles.
Beg with a k row cont in st st until front
measures 11¾(13¾:15½:17)in/30(35:39:43)cm
from cast on edge, ending with a k row.

**Shape shoulder**
Bind off 11(12:13:14) sts at beg of next row.
Work 1 row.
Bind off rem 12(13:14:14) sts.

**SLEEVES**
With US 6 (4mm) needles cast on
38(42:42:46) sts.
1st row K2, ★ p2, k2; rep from ★ to end.
2nd row P2, ★ k2, p2; rep from ★ to end
Rep the last 2 rows for 2in/5cm, ending with
a 2nd row.
Change to US 5 (3¾mm) needles.
Work a further 2in/5cm in rib, ending with a
2nd row, inc 6 sts evenly across last row.
44(48:48:52) sts.
Change to US 6 (4mm) needles.
Beg with a k row, work in st st, inc one st at
each end of the 3rd and every foll 4th row
until there are 58(64:68:74) sts.
Cont straight until sleeve measures
9(10:11:12¼)in/23(25:28:31)cm from cast on
edge, ending with a p row.
Bind off.

**FRONTBANDS AND COLLAR**
Join shoulder seams.
With US 5 (3¾mm) needles and right side facing, pick up
and k71(82:93:101) sts up right front to shoulder seam,
20(22:24:28) sts from back neck, 71(82:93:101) sts down left
front. 162(186:210:230) sts.
1st row P2, ★ k2, p2; rep from ★ to end.
This row sets the rib.
Next 2 rows Rib to last 65(75:86:94) sts, turn.
Next 2 rows Rib to last 59(69:79:87) sts, turn.
Next 2 rows Rib to last 53(63:72:80) sts, turn.
Next 2 rows Rib to last 47(57:65:73) sts, turn.
Next row Rib to end.
Rib 3 more rows.
Buttonhole row Rib 4, [work 2 tog, yf, rib 14(16:14:16)]
2(2:3:3) times, work 2 tog, yf, rib to end.
Rib 13(15:17:19) more rows.

**Divide for collar shaping**
Next row Rib 59(68:77:84), turn.
Rib 3 rows.
Rep the buttonhole row.
Rib 5 more rows.
Bind off in rib.
With US 5 (3¾mm) needles and right side facing, rejoin yarn
to rem sts, rib 44(50:56:62) sts, turn.
Rib 9 rows.

Bind off in rib.
With US 5 (3¾mm) needles and right side facing, rejoin yarn to rem sts, rib to end.
Rib 9 rows.
Bind off in rib.

### FINISH

With center of sleeves to shoulder seam, sew on sleeves. Join side and sleeve seams.
Sew on buttons.

### HAT
### TO MAKE

With US 6 (4mm) needles cast on 82(90) sts.
**1st rib row** K2, ★ p2, k2; rep from ★ to end.
**2nd rib row** P2, ★ k2, p2; rep from ★ to end.
Rep the last 2 rows until hat measures 6¼(7)in./16(18)cm from cast on edge, ending with a 2nd rib row.

### Shape top

**1st row** K2, ★p2 tog, k2; rep from ★ to end. 62(68)sts.
**2nd row** P2, ★ k1, p2; rep from ★ to end.
**3rd row** K2, ★ p1, k2; rep from ★ to end.
**4th row** P2, ★ k1, p2; rep from ★ to end.
**5th row** K2 tog, ★p1, k2 tog; rep from ★ to end. 41(45) sts.
**6th row** P1, ★ k1, p1; rep from ★ to end.
**7th row** K1, ★ p3 tog, k1; rep from ★ to end. 21(23) sts.
**8th row** P1, ★ p2 tog; rep from ★ to end.
Break off yarn, thread end through rem sts, pull up and secure.
Join seam. Make a small pom-pom and sew to crown.

# BUTTERFLY bag

A cute bag with a butterfly motif which has decorative beads sewn on afterwards, rather than using the knitted-in technique. You could use sparkly, crystal beads for a more special look for a grown-up evening bag.

**Materials**

One 50g ball of Debbie Bliss cotton double knitting in Main Color (M) and small amount each of Red and Turquoise. Pair of US 6 (4mm) needles. 200 red beads.

**Measurements**

6¾in x 4¼in/17cm x 11cm.

**Gauge**

20 sts and 28 rows to 4in/10cm square over st st using US 6 (4mm) needles.

**Abbreviations**

See page 127.

**Note**

Read chart from right to left on right side rows and from left to right on wrong side rows (see page 113). Use separate balls of yarn for each area of color and twist yarns together on wrong side to avoid holes (see page 116).

**MAIN PART**

With US 6 (4mm) needles and M cast on 31 sts.
K 2 rows.
Beg with a p row work 28 rows in st st, ending with a k row.
K 1 row.
Beg with a k row work 5 rows in st st.
K 1 row.

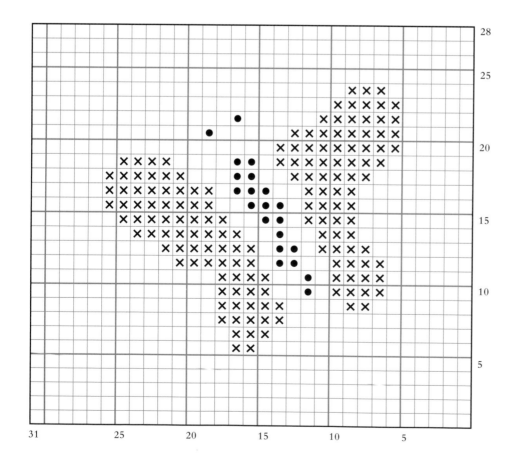

**Key**

☐ Navy
● Red
☒ Turquoise

Beg with a k row work chart until 28th row is completed.
Cont in M.
K 2 rows.
Bind off.

**STRAP (MAKE ONE)**
With US 6 (4mm) needles and M cast on 6 sts.
Cont in garter st until strap measures 16½in/42cm. Bind off.

**FINISH**
Place cast on edge of strap between two garter st ridges in
middle of bag and bound off edge on other side between
two garter st ridges. Sew into place. Sew side edges of bag to
row ends of straps. Sew beads onto butterfly shape randomly
using picture as guide.

# GUERNSEY dress

This pretty dress for a baby is inspired by traditional fisherman or Guernsey sweaters. The patterned yoke is a patchwork of neat cables, seed-stitch hearts, and lace and bobbles. There are also matching bootees, see page 46, and a throw, see page 82.

## Materials

5(6:8) 50g balls of Debbie Bliss wool/cotton.
Pair each of US 2 (3mm) and US 3 (3¼mm) knitting needles. Cable needle.
1st size only 3 buttons.

## Measurements

| To fit ages | 6-12 | 12-18 | 24-36 | months. |
|---|---|---|---|---|
| *Actual measurements* | | | | |
| Chest | 22 | 25¼ | 27½ | in |
|  | 56 | 64 | 70 | cm |
| Length to shoulder | 14¼ | 15¾ | 17¾in | in |
|  | 36 | 40 | 45 | cm |
| Sleeve length | 7 | 8 | 8¾ | in |
|  | 18 | 20 | 22 | cm |

## Gauge

25 sts and 34 rows to 4in/10cm square over st st using US 3 (3¼mm) needles.

## Abbreviations

**Mb** – work k1, p1, k1, p1, k1, into next st, turn, p5, turn, pass 2nd, 3rd, 4th and 5th st over first and off the needle, then pass st back onto right hand needle.
**C4F** – slip next 2 sts onto cable needle and hold at front of work, k2, then k2 from cable needle.
Also see pages 118 and 127.

## PANEL A

(worked over 15 sts)
**1st row** K to end.
**2nd row** P to end.
**3rd row** K7, p1, k7.
**4th row** P6, k1, p1, k1, p6.
**5th row** K5, p1, [k1, p1] twice, k5.
**6th row** P4, k1, [p1, k1] 3 times, p4.
**7th row** K3, p1, [k1, p1] 4 times, k3.
**8th row** P2, k1, [p1, k1] 5 times, p2.
**9th row** K1, [p1, k1] 7 times.
**10th row** As 8th row.
**11th row** As 9th row.
**12th row** As 8th row.
**13th row** [K1, p1] 3 times, k3, [p1, k1] 3 times.
**14th row** P2, k1, p1, k1, p5, k1, p1, k1, p2.
**15th row** K to end.
**16th row** P to end.

17th row K to end.
18th row P to end.
These 18 rows form the patt panel.

## PANEL B

(worked over 15 sts)
1st row K to end.
2nd and alt rows P to end.
3rd row K to end.
5th row K6, k2 tog, yf, k7.
7th row K5, k2 tog, yf, k1, yf, skpo, k5.
9th row K4, k2 tog, yf, k3, yf, skpo, k4.
11th row K3, k2 tog, yf, k2, Mb, k2, yf, skpo, k3.
13th row K2, k2 tog, yf, k7, yf, skpo, k2.
15th row K1, k2 tog, yf, k2, Mb, k3, Mb, k2, yf, skpo, k1.
17th row K to end.
18th row P to end.
These 18 rows form the patt panel.

*The Guernsey Dress and matching*
*Lace and Bobble Bootees.*

## PANEL C

(worked over 15 sts)
1st row K to end.
2nd and alt rows P to end.
3rd row K6, Mb, k2, [k2 tog, yf] twice, k2.
5th row K8, [k2 tog, yf] twice, k3.
7th row K7, [k2 tog, yf] twice, k4.
9th row K3, Mb, k2, [k2 tog, yf] twice, k5.
11th row K7, [yf, skpo] twice, k4.
13th row K8, [yf, skpo] twice, k3.
15th row K6, Mb, k2, [yf, skpo] twice, k2.
17th row K to end.
18th row P to end.
These 18 rows form the patt panel.

## PANEL D

(worked over 15 sts)
1st row K to end.
2nd and alt rows P to end.

**3rd row** K2, [yf, skpo] twice, k2, Mb, k6.
**5th row** K3, [yf, skpo] twice, k8.
**7th row** K4, [yf, skpo] twice, k7.
**9th row** K5, [yf, skpo] twice, k2, Mb, k3.
**11th row** K4, [k2 tog, yf] twice, k7.
**13th row** K3, [k2 tog, yf] twice, k8.
**15th row** K2, [k2 tog, yf] twice, k2, Mb, k6.
**17th row** K to end.
**18th row** P to end.
These 18 rows form the patt panel.

## BACK

With US 2 (3mm) needles cast on 105(117:127) sts.
**1st row (right side)** K1, *p1, k1; rep from * to end.
This row forms the seed st.
Work a further 5 rows.
Change to US 3 (3¼mm) needles.
Beg with a k row cont in st st until back measures
5½(6¾:8¼)in/14(17:21)cm from cast on edge, ending with a
k row.
**Dec row** P2(5:7), [p2 tog, p1] 33(35:37) times, p2 tog,
p2(5:7). 71(81:89) sts.
Cont in patt as folls:

*1st size only*
**1st row** * K1, [p1, k1] 10 times, C4F; rep from * once
more, k1, [p1, k1] 10 times.
**2nd row** * K1, [p1, k1] 10 times, p4; rep from * once more,
k1, [p1, k1] 10 times.
**3rd row** * K1, [p1, k1] 10 times, k4; rep from * once more,
k1, [p1, k1] 10 times.
**4th row** * K1, [p1, k1] 10 times, p4; rep from * once more,
k1, [p1, k1] 10 times.
These 4 rows form cable and seed st patt panel.
**5th row** Seed st 3, work 1st row of patt panel A, patt 10,
work 1st row of patt panel B, patt 10, work 1st row of patt
panel A, seed st 3.
**6th row** Seed st 3, work 2nd row of patt panel A, patt 10,
work 2nd row of patt panel B, patt 10, work 2nd row of patt
panel A, seed st 3.
**7th to 22nd rows** Rep 5th and 6th rows eight times,
working 3rd to 18th rows of patt panels.
**23rd row** * K1, [p1, k1] 10 times, k4; rep from * once
more, k1, [p1, k1] 10 times.
**24th row** * K1, [p1, k1] 10 times, p4; rep from * once more,
k1, [p1, k1] 10 times.
**25th row** * K1, [p1, k1] 10 times, C4F; rep from * once
more, k1, [p1, k1] 10 times.
**26th row** * K1, [p1, k1] 10 times, p4; rep from * once more,
k1, [p1, k1] 10 times.

**27th row** Seed st 3, work 1st row of patt
panel C, patt 10, work 1st row of patt panel
A, patt 10, work 1st row of patt panel D,
seed st 3.
**28th row** Seed st 3, work 2nd row of patt
panel D, patt 10, work 2nd row of patt panel
A, patt 10, work 2nd row of patt panel C,
seed st 3.
**29th to 44th rows** Rep 7th and 8th rows
eight times, working 3rd to 18th rows of
patt panels.
**45th row to 66th rows** As 1st to 22nd rows,
working p2 tog over each cable on last row.
69 sts.

*2nd size only*
**1st row** K1, C4F, * k1, [p1, k1] 10 times,
C4F; rep from * once more, [k1, p1] 10 times,
k1, C4F, k1.
**2nd row** K1, p4, * k1, [p1, k1] 10 times, p4;
rep from * once more, k1, [p1, k1] 10 times,
p4, k1.
**3rd row** K5, * k1, [p1, k1] 10 times, k4; rep
from * once more, [k1, p1] 10 times, k6.
**4th row** K1, p4, * k1, [p1, k1] 10 times, p4;
rep from * once more, k1, [p1, k1] 10 times,
p4, k1.
These 4 rows form cable and seed st
patt panel.
**5th row** Patt 8, work 1st row of patt panel A,
patt 10, work 1st row of patt panel B, patt 10,
work 1st row of patt panel A, patt 8.
**6th row** Patt 8, work 2nd row of patt panel
A, patt 10, work 2nd row of patt panel B, patt
10, work 2nd row of patt panel A, patt 8.
**7th to 22nd rows** Rep 5th and 6th rows
eight times, working 3rd to 18th rows of
patt panels.
**23rd row** K5, * k1, [p1, k1] 10 times, k4; rep
from * once more, [k1, p1] 10 times, k6.
**24th row** K1, p4, * k1, [p1, k1] 10 times, p4;
rep from * once more, k1, [p1, k1] 10 times,
p4, k1.
**25th row** K1, C4F, * k1, [p1, k1] 10 times,
C4F; rep from * once more, [k1, p1] 10 times,
k1, C4F, k1.
**26th row** K1, p4, * k1, [p1, k1] 10 times, p4;
rep from * once more, k1, [p1, k1] 10 times,
p4, k1.

**27th row** Patt 8, work 1st row of patt panel C, patt 10, work 1st row of patt panel A, patt 10, work 1st row of patt panel D, patt 8.

**28th row** Patt 8, work 2nd row of patt panel D, patt 10, work 2nd row of patt panel A, patt 10, work 2nd row of patt panel C, patt 8.

**29th to 44th rows** Rep 7th and 8th rows eight times, working 3rd to 18th rows of patt panels.

**45th row to 66th rows** As 1st to 22nd rows, working p2 tog over each cable on last row. 77 sts.

*3rd size only*

**1st row** P1, k1, C4F, ★ k1, [p1, k1] 11 times, C4F; rep from ★ once more, [k1, p1] 11 times, k1, C4F, k1, p1.

**2nd row** P1, k1, p4, ★ k1, [p1, k1] 11 times, p4; rep from ★ once more, k1, [p1, k1] 11 times, p4, k1, p1.

**3rd row** P1, k5, ★ k1, [p1, k1] 11 times, k4; rep from ★ once more, [k1, p1] 11 times, k6, p1.

**4th row** P1, k1, p4, ★ k1, [p1, k1] 11 times, p4; rep from ★ once more, k1, [p1, k1] 11 times, p4, k1, p1.

These 4 rows form cable and seed st patt panel.

**5th row** Patt 10, work 1st row of patt panel A, patt 12, work 1st row of patt panel B, patt 12, work 1st row of patt panel A, patt 10.

**6th row** Patt 10, work 2nd row of patt panel A, patt 12, work 2nd row of patt panel B, patt 12, work 2nd row of patt panel A, patt 10.

**7th to 22nd rows** Rep 5th and 6th rows eight times, working 3rd to 18th rows of patt panels.

**23rd row** P1, k5, ★ k1, [p1, k1] 11 times, k4; rep from ★ once more, [k1, p1] 11 times, k6, p1.

**24th row** P1, k1, p4, ★ k1, [p1, k1] 11 times, p4; rep from ★ once more, k1, [p1, k1] 11 times, p4, k1, p1.

**25th row** P1, k1, C4F, ★ k1, [p1, k1] 11 times, C4F; rep from ★ once more, [k1, p1] 11 times, k1, C4F, k1, p1.

**26th row** P1, k1, p4, ★ k1, [p1, k1] 11 times, p4; rep from ★ once more, k1, [p1, k1] 11 times, p4, k1, p1.

**27th row** Patt 10, work 1st row of patt panel C, patt 12, work 1st row of patt panel A, patt 12, work 1st row of patt panel D, patt 10.

**28th row** Patt 10, work 2nd row of patt panel D, patt 12, work 2nd row of patt panel A, patt 12, work 2nd row of patt panel C, patt 10.

**29th to 44th rows** Rep 7th and 8th rows eight times, working rows 3rd to 18th rows of patt panels.

**45th row to 66th rows** As 1st to 22nd rows, working p2 tog over each cable on last row. 85 sts.

*All sizes*

Work 17(21:25) rows seed st across all sts.

**Shape shoulders**

*1st size only*

**Buttonband**

**Next row** Seed st 20, turn.

Work 2 rows on these sts.

Bind off.

With wrong side facing, rejoin yarn to rem sts, patt to end.

**Next row** Bind off 20 sts, patt to end.

Leave rem sts on a holder.

*2nd and 3rd size only*

Bind off (23:26) sts at beg of next 2 rows.

Leave rem (31:33) sts on a holder.

**FRONT**

Work as given for Back until 66 rows have been worked in patt.

*All sizes*

Work 4 rows seed st across all sts.

**Shape neck**

**Next row** Patt 26(29:32) sts, turn and work on these sts for first side of front neck.

Dec one st at neck edge on next 6 rows. 20(23:26) sts.

Work 7(11:15) rows straight.

*1st size only*

**Buttonhole row** Seed st 4, yon, work 2 tog, seed st 8, yon, work 2 tog, seed st 4.

Work 2 rows seed st.

**All sizes**
**Shape shoulder**
Bind off.
With right side facing, slip center 17(19:21) sts on a holder, rejoin yarn to rem sts, patt to end.
Dec one st at neck edge on next 6 rows. 20(23:26) sts.
Work 6(10:14) rows straight.
Bind off.

**SLEEVES**
With US 2 (3mm) needles cast on 37(41:45) sts.
**1st row (right side)** K1, *p1, k1; rep from * to end.
This row forms the seed st.
Work a further 7 rows.
Change to US 3 (3¼mm) needles.
**Inc row** Seed st 3(5:7), [m1, seed st 10] 3 times, m1, seed st 4(6:8). 41(45:49) sts.
Cont in patt as folls:
**1st row** [K1, p1] 1(2:3) times, k4, * p1, [k1, p1] 3 times, k4; rep from * twice more, [p1, k1] 1(2:3) times.
**2nd row** K1, [p1, k1] 0(1:2) times, p6, * [k1, p1] twice, k1, p6; rep from * twice more, k1, [p1, k1] 0(1:2) times.

**3rd row** [K1, p1] 1(2:3) times, C4F, * p1, [k1, p1] 3 times, C4F; rep from * twice more, [p1, k1] 1(2:3) times.
**4th row** K1, [p1, k1] 0(1:2) times, p6, * [k1, p1] twice, k1, p6; rep from * twice more, k1, [p1, k1] 0(1:2) times.
These 4 rows **set** the position of cable and seed st patt panels.
Cont in patt, inc one st at each end of the next and every foll 4th row until there are 67(73:83) sts, working inc sts into seed st and cable patt.
Cont straight until sleeve measures 7(8:8¾)in/18(20:22)cm from cast on edge, ending with a wrong side row.
Bind off, working 2 sts tog over cables.

**NECKBAND**
Join right shoulder seam.
With right side facing using US 2 (3mm) needles, pick up and k14(12:14) sts down left front neck, k17(19:21) sts from center front holder, pick up and k9(11:13) sts up right front neck, k29(31:33) sts from center back holder, then for 1st size only pick up and k4 sts along buttonband.
73(73:81) sts.
**Next row** K1, * p1, k1; rep from * to end.
This row forms the seed st.

*1st size only*
**Next row** Patt 2, yon, work 2 tog, patt to end.

*All sizes*
Seed st 3(4:6) rows.
Bind off.

**FINISH**
*1st size only*
Lap buttonhole band over buttonband and catch side edges together. Sew on buttons.

*2nd and 3rd sizes only*
Join shoulder and neckband seam.

*All sizes*
Sew on sleeves. Join side and sleeve seams.

# LACE AND BOBBLE bootees

These bootees are designed to match the Guernsey Dress (page 40) and the Lace and Bobble Baby Throw (page 82).

## Materials
One 50g ball of Debbie Bliss wool/cotton. Pair of US 2 (2¾mm) knitting needles. 2 buttons.

## Measurements
To fit                    6 months.

## Gauge
25 sts and 34 rows to 4in/10cm square over st st using US 3 (3¼mm) needles.

## Abbreviations
**Mb** – work k1, p1, k1, p1, k1, into next st, turn, p5, turn, pass 2nd, 3rd, 4th and 5th st over first and off the needle, then pass st back onto right hand needle.
Also see page 127.

## RIGHT SHOE
With US 2 (2¾mm) needles cast on 34 sts.
K 1 row.
**1st row** K1, yf, k15, [yf, k1] twice, yf, k15, yf, k1.
**2nd row and 4 foll alt rows** K to end, working k1 tbl into yf of previous row.
**3rd row** K2, yf, k15, yf, k2, yf, k3, yf, k15, yf, k2.
**5th row** K3, yf, k15, [yf, k4] twice, yf, k15, yf, k3.
**7th row** K4, yf, k15, yf, k5, yf, k6, yf, k15, yf, k4.
**9th row** K5, yf, k15, [yf, k7] twice, yf, k15, yf, k5.
**11th row** K7, yf, [k9, yf] 5 times, k7. 65 sts.
**12th row** K to end, working k1 tbl into yf of previous row.
**Next row** K1, * p1, k1; rep from * to end.
Rep the last row 11 times more.

### Shape instep
**1st row** Patt 25, k14, skpo, turn.
**2nd row** Sl 1, p13, p2 tog, turn.
**3rd row** Sl 1, k5, k2 tog, yf, k6, skpo, turn.
**4th row** Sl 1, p13, p2 tog, turn.
**5th row** Sl 1, k4, k2 tog, yf, k1, yf, skpo, k4, skpo, turn.
**6th row** Sl 1, p13, p2 tog, turn.
**7th row** Sl 1, k3, k2 tog, yf, k3, yf, skpo, k3, skpo, turn.
**8th row** Sl 1, p13, p2 tog, turn.
**9th row** Sl 1, k2, k2 tog, yf, k2, Mb, k2, yf, skpo, k2, skpo, turn.
**10th row** Sl 1, p13, p2 tog, turn.
**11th row** Sl 1, k1, k2 tog, yf, k7, yf, skpo, k1, skpo, turn.
**12th row** Sl 1, p13, p2 tog, turn.
**13th row** Sl 1, k2 tog, yf, k2, Mb, k3, Mb, k2, yf, [skpo] twice, turn.
**14th row** Sl 1, p13, p2 tog, turn.
**15th row** Sl 1, k14, patt to end.
Bind off, dec one st at each corner.
Join sole and back seam.
With US 2 (2¾mm) needles, right side facing and beginning and ending within 8 sts of back seam, pick up and k15 sts evenly along heel.
**Next row** P1, * k1, p1; rep from * to end. **
**Next row** Cast on 3 sts, k1, p1, k1, patt to end, turn and cast on 19 sts.
**Next row** K1, * p1, k1; rep from * to end.
**Buttonhole row** Patt 33, yf, k2 tog, p1, k1.
Patt 2 rows.
Bind off.

## LEFT SHOE
Work as given for Right Shoe to **.
**Next row** Cast on 19 sts, k1, [p1, k1] 9 times, turn and cast on 3 sts.
**Next row** K1, * p1, k1; rep from * to end.
**Buttonhole row** K1, p1, k2 tog, yf, patt to end.
Patt 2 rows.
Bind off.

# BALLERINA TOP with flowers

A classic cross-over style that has been enhanced by adding a floral pattern and pretty lace edging. This design is a good introduction to the intarsia technique, as the motifs are not worked in an all-over pattern.

## BACK

With US 2 (2¾mm) needles and M cast on 81(86:91) sts.

K 9 rows.

Change to US 3 (3¼mm) needles.

Beg with a k row work 4 rows in st st.

**Next row** K4(5:6), ★ work 1st row of Chart, k7(8:9); rep from ★ to last 17(18:19) sts, work 1st row of Chart, k4(5:6).

**Next row** P4(5:6), ★ work 2nd row of Chart, p7(8:9); rep from ★ to last 17(18:19) sts, work 2nd row of Chart, p4(5:6).

These 2 rows set the patt

Cont in this way to end of Chart then work in M only, **at the same time** shape sides.

**Inc row** K3, m1, patt to last 3 sts, m1, k3.

Work 5 rows in patt.

Rep the last 6 rows 13 times more then inc row again. 111(116:121) sts.

Cont straight until back measures 11½(12¼:13)in/29(31:33)cm from cast on edge, ending with a p row.

## Shape armholes

Bind off 5 sts at beg of next 2 rows and 4 sts at beg of foll 2 rows.

**Next row** K3, skpo, k to last 5 sts, k2 tog, k3.

**Next row** P to end.

Rep the last 2 rows 7(8:9) times more. 77(80:83) sts.

Cont straight until back measures 18(19¼:20½)in/46(49:52)cm from cast on edge, ending with a p row.

## Materials

10(11:12) 50g balls of Debbie Bliss wool/cotton in Main Color (M) and one ball each of Pale Pink, Dark Pink, Light Green and Dark Green. Pair each of US 2 (2¾mm) and US 3 (3¼mm) needles.

## Measurements

| To fit | 32 | 34 | 36 | in |
|---|---|---|---|---|
| | 81 | 86 | 91 | cm |

*Actual measurements*

| Bust | 34¼ | 35¾ | 37½ | in |
|---|---|---|---|---|
| | 87 | 91 | 95 | cm |
| Length to shoulder | 18½ | 19¾ | 21 | in |
| | 47 | 50 | 53 | cm |
| Sleeve length | 13¾ | 14¼ | 14½ | in |
| | 35 | 36 | 37 | cm |

## Gauge

25 sts and 34 rows to 4in/10cm square over st st using US 3 (3¼mm) needles.

## Abbreviations

See page 127.

## Note

Read chart from right to left on right side rows and from left to right on wrong side rows (see page 113). When working color motifs, use separate lengths of contrast yarn for each colored area and twist yarns together on wrong side at joins to avoid holes, (see page 116).

**Shape neck**

**Next row** K23(24:25), turn and work on these sts for first side of neck.
Dec one st at neck edge on next 3 rows. 20(21:22) sts.

**Shape shoulder**

Bind off 10(11:11) sts at beg of next row.
Work 1 row.
Bind off rem 10(10:11) sts.
With right side facing, rejoin yarn to rem sts, bind off center 31(32:33) sts, k to end.
Complete to match first side.

**LEFT FRONT**

With US 2 (2¾mm) needles and M cast on 81(86:91) sts.
K 9 rows.
Change to US 3 (3¼mm) needles.
**Next row** K to end.
**Next row** K3, p to end.
Rep the last 2 rows once more.
**Next row** K4(5:6), ★ work 1st row of Chart, k7(8:9); rep from ★ to last 17(18:19) sts, work 1st row of Chart, k4(5:6).
**Next row** K3, p1(2:3), ★ work 2nd row of Chart, p7(8:9); rep from ★ to last 17(18:19) sts, work 2nd row of Chart, p4(5:6).
These 2 rows set the patt
Cont in this way to end of Chart then work in M only, **at the same time** shape sides.
**Inc row** K3, m1, patt to last 3 sts, m1, k3.
Work 5 rows in patt.
Rep the last 6 rows 3 times more then inc row again. 91(96:101) sts.
Work 2 rows.

**Shape neck**

**Next row** Bind off 5 sts, p to end.
**Next row** K to last 3 sts, k2 tog, k1.
**Next row** P to end.
**Next row** K3, m1, k to last 3 sts, k2 tog, k1.
**Next row** P to end.
Cont to dec at neck edge on every alt row **at the same time** cont to inc at side edge on every 6th row until 15 incs have been worked in all, then keep side edge straight until front measures 11½(12¼:13)in/29(31:33)cm from cast on edge, ending with a p row.

**Key**

- ☐ Main
- ◯ Pale Pink
- ● Dark Pink
- V Light Green
- ╱ Dark Green

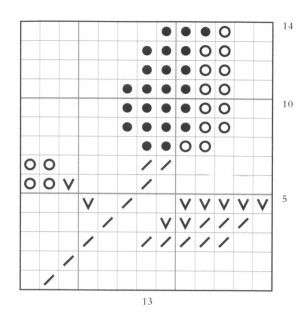

**Shape armhole**

**Next row** Bind off 5 sts, k to last 3 sts, k2 tog, k1.

**Next row** P to end.

**Next row** Bind off 4 sts, k to last 3 sts, k2 tog, k1.

**Next row** P to end.

**Next row** K3, skpo, k to last 3 sts, k2 tog, k1.

**Next row** P to end.

Rep the last 2 rows 7(8:9) times more.

Keeping armhole edge straight, cont to dec one st at neck edge on every alt row until 20(21:22) sts rem.

Work straight until front measures same as Back to shoulder shaping, ending at armhole edge.

**Shape shoulder**

Bind off 10(11:11) sts at beg of next row.

Work 1 row.

Bind off rem 10(10:11) sts.

**RIGHT FRONT**

With US 2 (2¾mm) needles and M cast on 81(86:91) sts.

K 9 rows.

Change to US 3 (3¼mm) needles.

**Next row** K to end.

**Next row** P to last 3 sts, k3.

Rep the last 2 rows once more.

**Next row** K4(5:6), ★ work 1st row of Chart, k7(8:9); rep from ★ to last 17(18:19) sts, work 1st row of Chart, k4(5:6).

**Next row** P4(5:6), ★ work 2nd row of Chart, p7(8:9); rep from ★ to last 17(18:19) sts, work 2nd row of Chart, p1(2:3), k3.

These 2 rows set the patt.

Cont in this way to end of Chart then work in M only, **at the same time** shape sides.

**Inc row** K3, m1, patt to last 3 sts, m1, k3.

Work 5 rows in patt.

Rep the last 6 rows 3 times more then the inc row again. 91(96:101) sts.

Work 1 row.

### Shape neck

**Next row** Bind off 5 sts, k to end.

**Next row** P to end.

**Next row** K to last 3 sts, k2 tog, k1.

**Next row** P to end.

**Next row** K1, skpo, k to last 3 sts, m1, k3.

**Next row** P to end.

Cont to dec at neck edge on every alt row **at the same time** cont to inc at side edge on every 6th row until 15 incs have been worked in all, then keep side edge straight until front measures 11½(12¼:13)in/29(31:33)cm from cast on edge, ending with a k row.

### Shape armhole

**Next row** Bind off 5 sts, p to end.

**Next row** K1, skpo, k to end.

**Next row** Bind off 4 sts, p to end.

**Next row** K1, skpo, k to last 5 sts, k2 tog, k3.

**Next row** P to end.

Rep the last 2 rows 7(8:9) times more.

Keeping armhole edge straight, cont to dec one st at neck edge on every alt row until 20(21:22) sts rem.

Work straight until front measures same as Back to shoulder shaping, ending at armhole edge.

### Shape shoulder

Bind off 10(11:11) sts at beg of next row.

Work 1 row.

Bind off rem 10(10:11) sts.

### SLEEVES

With US 2 (2¾mm) needles and M cast on 54(58:62) sts.

K 9 rows.

Change to US 3 (3¼mm) needles.

Work 2(4:6) rows st st.

**Inc row** K3, m1, k to last 3 sts, m1, k3.

Beg with a p row, cont in st st, inc one st at each end of every foll 8th row until there are 80(84:88) sts.

Cont straight until sleeve measures 13¾(14¼:14½)in/35(36:37)cm from cast on edge, ending with a p row.

### Shape sleeve top

Bind off 5 sts at beg of next 2 rows and 4 sts on foll 2 rows.

**Next row** K3, skpo, k to last 5 sts, k2 tog, k3.

**Next row** P to end.

**Next row** K to end.

**Next row** P to end.

Rep the last 4 rows 3(3:4) times more and the first 2 rows 0(1:0) times. 54(56:60) sts.

Bind off.

### LACE EDGING

With US 2 (2¾mm) needles and M cast on 4 sts.

K 1 row.

**1st row (right side)** K2, yf, k2.

**2nd row and 2 foll alt rows** Sl 1, k to end.

**3rd row** K3, yf, k2.

**5th row** K2, yf, k2 tog, yf, k2.

**7th row** K3, yf, k2 tog, yf, k2.

**8th row** Bind off 4 sts, k to end.

Rep the last 8 rows until edging, when slightly stretched, fits around neck edge, starting and ending at side edge.

### TIES (MAKE 2)

With US 2 (2¾mm) needles and M cast on 5 sts.

Cont in garter st until tie measures 29in/74cm. Bind off.

### FINISH

Join shoulder seams. Sew on sleeves. Sew ties to fronts level with beg of neck shaping. Join side and sleeve seams, leaving small opening in right seam level with neck shaping. Sew edging in place.

# TUNIC WITH contrast edging

An ideal design for inexperienced knitters who want to introduce some color into a project, without embarking on complicated Fair Isle or intarsia. The simple stockinette stitch tunic is enlivened with contrast borders and pocket linings.

## Materials

6(7:9) 50g balls of Debbie Bliss cotton double knitting in Main Color (M). One ball each of three Contrast Colors, Purple (A), Red (B) and Green (C) Pair each of US 5 (3¾mm) and US 6 (4mm) knitting needles.

## Measurements

| To fit ages | 1 | 2 | 3 | years. |
|---|---|---|---|---|
| *Actual measurements* | | | | |
| Chest | 25¼ | 28½ | 31½ | in |
| | 64 | 72 | 80 | cm |
| Length to shoulder | 14¼ | 15¾ | 18 | in |
| | 36 | 40 | 46 | cm |
| Sleeve length | 7½ | 8¾ | 10 | in |
| | 19 | 22 | 25 | cm |

## Gauge

20 sts and 28 rows to 4in/10cm square over st st using US 6 (4mm) needles.

## Abbreviations

See page 127.

## BACK

With US 5 (3¾mm) needles and A cast on 66(74:82) sts.

**1st row** K2, ★ p2, k2; rep from ★ to end.

**2nd row** P to end.

Rep the last 2 rows 5(6:7) times more.

Change to 4mm (US 6) needles and M.

Beg with a k row, cont in st st until back measures 8(9:10¼)in/20(23:26)cm from cast on edge, ending with a p row.

### Shape armholes

Bind off 5 sts at beg of next 2 rows. 56(64:72) sts.

Cont in st st until back measures 13½(15:17¼)in/34(38:44)cm from cast on edge, ending with a p row.

### Shape Neck

**Next row** K20(23:26) turn and work on these sts for first side of back neck.

Dec one st at neck edge on next 4 rows. 16(19:22) sts

Work 1 row straight.

### Shape shoulder

Bind off 8(9:11) sts at beg of next row.

Work 1 row.

Bind off rem 8(10:11) sts.

With right side facing, slip center 16(18:20) sts onto a holder, join on yarn, k to end.

Complete to match first side of neck.

**Shape armholes**

Bind off 5 sts at beg of next 2 rows. 56(64:72) sts.

Cont in st st until front measures 12½(13¾:15¾)in/32(35:40)cm from cast on edge, ending with a p row.

**Shape Neck**

Next row K22(25:28) turn and work on these sts for first side of front neck.

Dec one st at neck edge on every row until 16(19:22) sts rem.

Work straight until front measures same as Back to shoulder, ending at armhole edge.

**Shape shoulder**

Bind off 8(9:11) sts at beg of next row.

Work 1 row.

Bind off rem 8(10:11) sts.

With right side facing, slip centre 12(14:16) sts onto a holder, join on yarn, k to end. Complete to match first side of neck.

**POCKET LININGS (MAKE 2)**

With US 6 (4mm) needles and B cast on 18(22:22) sts.

Beg with a k row work 19(21:23) rows in st st, ending with a k row.

Leave these sts on a spare needle.

**FRONT**

With US 5 (3¾mm) needles and A cast on 66(74:82) sts.

**1st row** K2, ★ p2, k2; rep from ★ to end.

**2nd row** P to end.

Rep the last 2 rows 5(6:7) times more.

Change to US 6 (4mm) needles and M.

Beg with a k row, work 18(20:22) rows in st st, ending with a p row.

**Place pocket**

Next row K7(7:9) sts, k next 18(22:22) sts and leave these sts on a holder, k16(16:20), k next 18(22:22) sts and leave these sts on a holder, k last 7(7:9) sts.

Next row P7(7:9) sts, p across 18(22:22) sts of one pocket lining, p16(16:20), p across 18(22:22) sts of second pocket lining, p7(7:9).

Beg with a k row, cont in st st until front measures 8(9:10¼)in/20(23:26)cm from cast on edge, ending with a p row.

**SLEEVES**

With US 5 (3¾mm) needles and C, cast on 30(34:38) sts.

Work 9(11:13) rows rib as given for back.

**Inc row** P2(4:6), m1, [p5, m1] 5 times, p3(5:7). 36(40:44) sts.

Change to US 6 (4mm) needles and M.

Beg with a k row, cont in st st, inc one st at each end of every 3rd row until there are 64(70:78) sts.

Work straight until sleeve measures 7½(8¾:10)in/19(22:25)cm from cast on edge, ending with a p row.

Work a further 8 rows. Bind off.

**NECKBAND**

Join right shoulder seam.

With right side facing, US 5 (3¾mm) needles and B, pick up and k14 sts down left side of front neck, k across 12(14:16) sts from front neck holder, pick up and k14 sts up right side of front neck, 7 sts from right back neck, k16(18:20) across sts from back neck holder, pick up and k 7 sts from left back neck. 70(74:78) sts.

**1st row** P2. ★ k2, p2; rep from ★ to end.

**2nd row** K to end.

Rep the last 2 rows 3 times more.

Change to US 6 (4mm) needles.

**1st row** K to end.
**2nd row** P2. ★ k2, p2; rep from ★ to end.
Rep the last 2 rows 3 times more and the 1st row again.
Bind off in rib.

**POCKET TOPS**
With right side facing, US 5 (3¾mm) needles and C, k across 18(22:22) sts of pocket front.
**1st row** P2. ★ k2, p2; rep from ★ to end.
**2nd row** K to end.
**3rd row** P2. ★ k2, p2; rep from ★ to end.
Bind off.

**TO FINISH**
Join left shoulder and neckband seam, reversing final 9 rows to fold over. Sew on sleeves, sew last 8 rows to sts bind off at under arm. Join side and sleeve seams. Sew down pocket linings and pocket tops.

# ZIPPED JACKET with hood

A good, all-year-round jacket with a cabled yoke and hood. There are no increasings before the yoke, giving it the slightly A-line shape that I love on small children, while the zip gives it a sporty edge.

## Materials

11(12:13) 50g balls of Debbie Bliss cotton double knitting. Pair each of US 5 (3¾mm) and US 6 (4mm) knitting needles. Cable needle. 14(16:18)in/ 35(40·45)cm open-ended zip.

## Measurements

| To fit ages | 2-3 | 4-5 | 6-7 | years. |
|---|---|---|---|---|
| *Actual measurements* | | | | |
| Chest | 31½ | 37 | 42½ | in |
| | 80 | 94 | 108 | cm |
| Length to shoulder | 15¾ | 17¾ | 19¾ | in |
| | 40 | 45 | 50 | cm |
| Sleeve length | 10 | 10½ | 11¾ | in |
| | 25 | 27 | 30 | cm |

## Gauge

20 sts and 28 rows to 4in/10cm square over st st using US 6 (4mm) needles.
21 sts and 30 rows to 4in/10cm square over cable patt using US 6 (4mm) needles.

## Abbreviations

**C4F** – slip next 2 sts onto cable needle and leave at front, k2, then k2 from cable needle.
**C4B** – slip next 2 sts onto cable needle and leave at back, k2, then k2 from cable needle.
See pages 118 and 127.

## BACK

With US 5 (3¾mm) needles cast on 84(99:114) sts.
K 2 rows.
Change to US 6 (4mm) needles.
Beg with a k row, cont in st st until back measures 8(9:10¼)in/20(23:26)cm, ending with a p row.
Cont in yoke patt:
**Next row** *[P1, k1] 4 times, p1, k2, C4F; rep from * to last 9 sts, [p1, k1] 4 times, p1.
**Next row** P1, * k1, p5, k1, p8; rep from * to last 8 sts, k1, p5, k1, p1.
**Next row** *[P1, k1] 4 times, p1, C4B, k2; rep from * to last 9 sts, [p1, k1] 4 times, p1.
**Next row** P1, * k1, p5, k1, p8; rep from * to last 8 sts, k1, p5, k1, p1.
Rep last 4 rows until back measures 15¾(17¾:19¾)in/40(45:50)cm, ending with a wrong side row.

### Shape shoulders

Bind off 12(14:16) sts at the beg of the next 4 rows.
Bind off rem 36(43:50) sts.

## LEFT FRONT

With US 5 (3¾mm) needles cast on 40(49:55) sts.
**1st row** K to last 4 sts, [p1, k1] twice.
**2nd row** [K1, p1] twice, k to end.
Change to US 6 (4mm) needles.
**3rd row** K to last 4 sts, [p1, k1] twice.
**4th row** K1, p1, k1, p to end.
Keeping 4 edge sts in seed st and the rem sts

in st st work 8(10:12) rows, ending with a
wrong side row.

**Shape pocket**

**Next row** K12(14:16) sts, turn and place rem
sts on a holder, cast on 24(26:28) sts. 36(40:44)
sts.

Beg with a p row work 29(31:33) rows st st.
Leave these sts on a spare needle.

With right side facing, rejoin yarn to sts at
center front.

**Next row** K to last 4 sts, [p1, k1] twice.

**Next row** K1, p1, k1, p to last 2 sts, k2.

Rep the last 2 rows 14(15:16) times more,
ending with a wrong side row.

Return to first set of sts on holder.

K the first 12(14:16) sts, place the pocket
lining behind sts of front, then [k next st on
front tog with next st from pocket lining]
24(26:28) times, patt to end.

Keeping the edge 4 sts in seed st and rem sts
in st st, work until front measures
8(9:10¼)in/20(23:26)cm, ending with a wrong
side row.

**Next row** *P1, [k1, p1] 4 times, k2, C4F;
rep from * 1(2:2) times, p1, [k1, p1] 4(1:4)
times, k1.

**Next row** K1, p1, [k1, p8] 0(1:0) times, [k1,
p5, k1, p8] 2(2:3) times, k1, p5, k1, p1.

**Next row** *P1, [k1, p1] 4 times, C4B, k2;
rep from * 1(2:2) times, p1, [k1, p1] 4(1:4)
times, k1.

**Next row** K1, p1, [k1, p8] 0 (1, 0) times [k1,
p5, k1, p8] 2(2:3) times, k1, p5, k1, p1.

Rep the last 4 rows until left front measures
13¾(15¾:17¾)in/35(40:45)cm, ending with a
right side row.

**Shape neck**

**Next row** Bind off 7(9:11) sts, work to end.
Dec one st at neck edge on every row until
24(28:32) sts rem.

Work straight until front matches Back to
shoulder shaping, ending at side edge.

**Shape shoulder**

Bind off 12(14:16) sts at the beg of the
next row.
Work 1 row.
Bind off rem 12(14:16) sts

**RIGHT FRONT**

Using US 5 (3¾mm) needles cast on 40(49:55) sts.

**1st row** P1, k1, p1, k to end

**2nd row** K to last 3 sts p1, k1, p1.

Change to US 6 ( 4mm) needles.

**3rd row** P1, k1, p1, k to end.

**4th row** P to last 4 sts, [k1, p1] twice.

Keeping 4 edge sts in seed st and the rem sts in st st work
8(10:12) rows, ending with a wrong side row.

**Shape pocket**

**Next row** Patt 28(35:39), turn and place rem sts on a
spare needle.

**Next row** P to last 4 sts, [k1, p1] twice.

Work a further 28(30:32) rows as set.

Leave these sts on a spare needle.

Return to first set of sts on spare needle.

Cast on 24(26:28) sts, k these sts, then with right side facing,
k across sts on spare needle.

Beg with a p row, work 29(31:33) rows in st st.

With right side facing, rejoin yarn to sts at center front.

Patt the first 4(9:11) sts, place the pocket lining behind sts of
front, then [k next st on front tog with next st from pocket
lining] 24(26:28) times, k to end.

Keeping the edge 4 sts in seed st and rem sts in st st, work
until front measures 8(9:10¼)in/20(23:26)cm, ending with a
wrong side row.

**Next row** [K1, p1] 5(2:5) times, * k2, C4F, [p1, k1] 4 times,
p1; rep from *1(2:2) times.

**Next row** P1, k1, p5, * k1, p8, k1, p5; rep from * 1(1:2)
times, k1, p1(8:1), k1, p0(1:0), k0(1:0).

**Next row** [K1, p1] 5(2:5) times, * C4B, k2, [p1, k1] 4 times,
p1; rep from *1(2:2) times.

**Next row** P1, k1, p5, * k1, p8, k1, p5; rep from * 1(1:2)
times, k1, p1(8:1), k1, p0(1:0), k0(1:0).

Rep the last 4 rows until right front measures
13¾(15¾:17¾)in/35(40:45cm), ending with a wrong side row.

**Shape neck**

**Next row** Bind off 7(9:11) sts, work to end.
Dec one st at neck edge on every row until 24(28:32)
sts rem.
Work straight until front matches Back to shoulder shaping,
ending at side edge.

**Shape shoulder**

Bind off 12(14:16) sts at the beg of the next row.
Work 1 row.
Bind off rem 12(14:16) sts

## SLEEVES

With US 5 (3¾mm) needles cast on 44(52:60) sts.

K 2 rows.

Change to US 6 (4mm) needles.

Cont in patt.

**1st row** K1(1:3), p1, [k1, p1] 1(3:4) times, ★ k2, C4F, p1, [k1, p1] 4 times; rep from ★ once more, k2, C4F, [p1, k1] 1(3.4) times, p1, k1(1:3).

**2nd row** P0(0:4), k0(1:1), p2(5:5), ★ k1, p8, k1, p5; rep from ★ once more, k1, p8, k1, p2(5:5), k0(1:1), p0(0:4).

**3rd row** K1(1:3), p1, [k1, p1] 1(3:4) times, ★ C4B, k2, p1, [k1, p1] 4 times; rep from ★ once more, C4B, k2, [p1, k1] 1(3:4) times, p1, k1(1:3).

**4th row** P0(0:4), k0(1:1), p2(5:5), ★ k1, p8, k1, p5; rep from ★ once more, k1, p8, k1, p2(5:5), k0(1:1), p0(0:4).

These 4 rows set the patt.

Cont in patt **at the same time** inc one st at each end of next and every foll 4th row until there are 82(92:102) sts.

Cont straight until sleeve measures 10(10½:11¾)in/25(27:30)cm from cast on edge ending with a wrong side row.

Bind off.

## HOOD

Join shoulder seams.

With US 6 (4mm) needles and right side facing, pick up and k22(28:34) sts along left front neck, 37(43:51) sts across back neck, 22(28:34) sts along right front neck. 81(99:119) sts.

**Next row:** K2, p1, [k1, p1] to last 2 sts, k2.

Rep the last row until hood measures 9½(10½:11½)in/24(27:29)cm dec one st at center of last row.

**Next row** Patt 40(49:59) sts, with right sides tog, fold hood in half and bind off the sts of the hood tog by knitting into the first st on one needle and the first st on the other needle, k tog until 2 sts are on the right hand needle, bind off one st, cont until all sts are bound off.

## FINISH

Sew on sleeves, placing center of sleeves to shoulder seams. Join side and sleeve seams. Sew in zip. Sew down pocket linings.

# CABLE SWEATER **with pocket**

This classic long-line aran sweater contrasts cables and bobbles with a deep welt in a subtle chevron pattern. The pocket, borders and cuffs are edged with pale blue. This design is for the more experienced knitter.

### Materials

10(12) 50g balls of Debbie Bliss cotton double knitting in Main Color (M). One ball in Contrast Color (C). Pair each of US 3 (3¼mm) and US 6 (4mm) knitting needles. Cable needle.

### Measurements

| To fit ages | 3-5 | 5-7 | years. |
|---|---|---|---|
| *Actual measurements* | | | |
| Chest | 33¾ | 37 | in |
| | 86 | 94 | cm |
| Length to shoulder | 16½ | 17¾ | in |
| | 42 | 45 | cm |
| Sleeve length | 10 | 11¾ | in |
| | 25 | 30 | cm |

### Gauge

20 sts and 28 rows to 4in/10cm square over st st using US 6 (4mm) needles.

### Abbreviations

**C6B** – slip next 3 sts onto cable needle and hold at back of work, k3, then k3 from cable needle.
**Cr2L** – slip next st onto cable needle and hold at front of work, p1, then k1 from cable needle.
**Cr2R** – slip next st onto cable needle and hold at back of work, k1, then p1 from cable needle.
**C2B** – slip next st onto cable needle and hold at back of work, k1, then k1b from cable needle.
**C2F** – slip next st onto cable needle and hold at front of work, k1b, then k1 from cable needle.
**C4B** – slip next 2 sts onto cable needle and hold at back of work, k2, then k2 from cable needle.
**C4F** – slip next 2 sts onto cable needle and hold at front of work, k2, then k2 from cable needle.
**k1b** – knit into back of st.
**p1b** – purl into back of st.
**Mb** – work k1, p1, k1 and p1, into next st, turn, p4, turn, [k2 tog] twice, pass 2nd st over first and off the needle.
See also pages 118 and 127.

### PANEL A

(worked over 11 sts)
**1st row** P3, Cr2R, k1b, Cr2L, p3.
**2nd row** K3, p1, [k1, p1] twice, k3.
**3rd row** P2, C2B, p1, k1b, p1, C2F, p2.
**4th row** K2, p2, k1, p1, k1, p2, k2.
**5th row** P1, Cr2R, k1b, [p1, k1b] twice, Cr2L, p1.
**6th row** K1, [p1, k1] 5 times.

7th row P1, Cr2L, k1b, [p1, k1b] twice, Cr2R, p1.

8th row As 4th row.

9th row P2, Cr2L, p1, k1b, p1, Cr2R, p2.

10th row As 2nd row.

11th row P3, Cr2L, k1b, Cr2R, p3.

12th row K4, p3, k4.

13th row P4, sl next 2 sts onto cable needle and leave at back of work, k1, then k1b, k1, from cable needle, p4.

14th row K4, p3, k4.

These 14 rows form the patt and are repeated throughout.

**PANEL B**

(worked over 18 sts)

1st row P4, Cr2R, k6, Cr2L, p4.

2nd row K4, p1b, k1, p6, k1, p1b, k4.

3rd row P3, Cr2R, p1, k6, p1, Cr2L, p3.

4th row K3, p1b, k2, p6, k2, p1b, k3.

5th row P2, Cr2R, p2, C6B, p2, Cr2L, p2.

6th row K2, p1b, k3, p6, k3, p1b, k2.

7th row P1, Cr2R, p3, k6, p3, Cr2L, p1.

8th row K1, p1b, k4, p6, k4, p1b, k1.

9th row P1, Cr2L, p3, k6, p3, Cr2R, p1.

10th row As 6th row.

11th row P2, Cr2L, p2, C6B, p2, Cr2R, p2.

12th row As 4th row.

13th row P3, Cr2L, p1, k6, p1, Cr2R, p3.

14th row As 2nd row.

15th row P4, Cr2L, k6, Cr2R, p4.

16th row K5, p1b, p6, p1b, k5.

These 16 rows form the patt and are repeated throughout.

**PANEL C**

(worked over 39 sts)

1st row P7, ★ [Cr2R] twice, p1, [Cr2L] twice, p7; rep from ★ once more.

2nd row K7, ★ p1b, k1, p1b, k3, p1b, k1, p1b, k7; rep from ★ once more.

3rd row P6, ★ [Cr2R] twice, p3, [Cr2L] twice, p5; rep from ★ once more, p1.

4th row K6, ★ p1b, k1, p1b, k5; rep from ★ 3 times more, k1.

5th row P5, ★ [Cr2R] twice, p5, [Cr2L] twice, p3; rep from ★ once more, p2.

6th row K5, ★ p1b, k1, p1b, k7, p1b, k1, p1b, k3; rep from ★

once more, k2.

**7th row** P4, ★ [Cr2R] twice, p7, [Cr2L] twice, p1; rep from ★ once more, p3.

**8th row** K4, ★ p1b, k1, p1b, k9, [p1b, k1] twice; rep from ★ once more, k3.

**9th row** P3, Mb, ★ k1, p1, k1, p9, k1 p1, k1, Mb; rep from ★ once more, p3.

**10th row** As 8th row.

**11th row** P4, ★ [Cr2L] twice, p7, [Cr2R] twice, p1; rep from ★ once more, p3.

**12th row** As 6th row.

**13th row** P5, ★ [Cr2L] twice, p5, [Cr2R] twice, p3; rep from ★ once more, p2.

**14th row** As 4th row.

**15th row** P6, ★ [Cr2L] twice, p3, [Cr2R] twice, p5; rep from ★ once more, p1.

**16th row** As 2nd row.

**17th row** P7, ★ [Cr2L] twice, p1, [Cr2R] twice, p7; rep from ★ once more.

**18th row** K8, ★ p1b, [k1, p1b] 3 times, k9, p1b, [k1, p1b] 3 times, k8.

**19th row** P8, k1, p1, k1, Mb, k1, p1, k1, p9, k1, p1, k1, Mb, k1, p1, k1, p8.

**20th row** As 18th row.

These 20 rows form the patt and are repeated throughout.

## BACK

With US 3 (3¼mm) needles and C, cast on 111(123) sts.

**1st row** K3, ★ p2, Cr2R, k1, Cr2L, p2, k3; rep from ★ to end.

**2nd row** P3, ★ k2, p1, [k1, p1] twice, k2, p3; rep from ★ to end.

Cont in M only.

**3rd row** K3, ★ p1, Cr2R, p1, k1, p1, Cr2L, p1, k3; rep from ★ to end.

**4th row** P3, ★ k1, p1, [k2, p1] twice, k1, p3; rep from ★ to end.

**5th row** K3, ★ Cr2R, p2, k1, p2, Cr2L, k3; rep from ★ to end.

**6th row** P3, ★ k4, p1, k4, p3; rep from ★ to end.

These 6 rows form the welt patt.

Cont in patt until 36 rows have been worked, inc one st at each end of last row. 113(125) sts.

Change to US 6 (4mm) needles and patt.

*1st size only*

**1st row** Work across 1st row of panel A, k4, work across 1st row of panel B, k4, work across 1st row of panel C, k4, work across 1st row of panel B, k4, work across 1st row of panel A.

**2nd row** Work across 2nd row of panel A, p4, work across 2nd row of panel B, p4, work across 2nd row of panel C, p4, work across 2nd row of panel B, p4, work across 2nd row of panel A.

**3rd row** Work across 3rd row of panel A, C4F, work across 3rd row of panel B, C4F, work across 3rd row of panel C, C4B, work across 3rd row of panel B, C4B, work across 3rd row of panel A.

**4th row** Work across 4th row of panel A, p4, work across 4th row of panel B, p4, work across 4th row of panel C, p4, work across 4th row of panel B, p4, work across 4th row of panel A.

These 4 rows form cable panels and set the patt for panels A, B, and C.

*2nd size only*

**1st row** P2, k4, work across 1st row of panel A, k4, work across 1st row of panel B, k4, work across 1st row of panel C, k4, work across 1st row of panel B, k4, work across 1st row of panel A, k4, p2.

**2nd row** K2, p4, work across 2nd row of panel A, p4, work across 2nd row of panel B, p4, work across 2nd row of panel C, p4, work across 2nd row of panel B, p4, work across 2nd row of panel A, p4, k2.

**3rd row** P2, C4F, work across 3rd row of panel A, C4F, work across 3rd row of panel B, C4F, work across 3rd row of panel C, C4B, work across 3rd row of panel B, C4B, work across 3rd row of panel A, C4B, p2.

**4th row** K2, p4, work across 4th row of panel A, p4, work across 4th row of panel B, p4, work across 4th row of panel C, p4, work across 4th row of panel B, p4, work across 4th row of panel A, p4, k2.

These 4 rows form cable panels and set the patt for panels A, B, and C.

*Both sizes*

Patt a further 80(90) rows.

**Shape neck**

**Next row** Patt 43(47) sts, turn and work on these sts for first side of neck.

Bind off 3 sts at beg of next and foll alt row. 37(41) sts.

**Shape shoulder**
Bind off 12(13) sts at beg of next and foll
alt row.
Work 1 row.
Bind off rem 13(15) sts.
With right side facing, slip center 27(31) sts
onto a holder, rejoin yarn to rem sts, patt
to end.
Complete to match first side.

**POCKET LINING (MAKE 1)**
With US 3 (3¼mm) needles and M, cast on
27 sts.
Starting with a k row, work 35 rows in st st.
Leave these sts on a holder.

**FRONT**
With US 3 (3¼mm) needles and C, cast on
111(123) sts.
**1st row** K3, ★ p2, Cr2R, k1, Cr2L, p2, k3; rep
from ★ to end.
**2nd row** P3, ★ k2, p1, [k1, p1] twice, k2, p3;
rep from ★ to end.
Cont in M only.
**3rd row** K3, ★ p1, Cr2R, p1, k1, p1, Cr2L, p1,
k3; rep from ★ to end.
**4th row** P3, ★ k1, p1, [k2, p1] twice, k1, p3;
rep from ★ to end.
**5th row** K3, ★ Cr2R, p2, k1, p2, Cr2L, k3; rep
from ★ to end.
**6th row** P3, ★ k4, p1, k4, p3; rep from ★
to end.
These 6 rows form the welt patt.
Cont in patt until 34 rows have been worked.
**Next row** Patt 72(84) sts in M, patt 27 sts in
C, patt 12 sts in M.
**Next row** Using M, inc in first st, patt next
11 sts, patt next 27 sts in C and place these
27 sts on a spare needle, using M, p across sts
of pocket lining, then patt 71(83) sts, inc in
last st. 113(125) sts.
Change to US 6 (4mm) needles and patt as
given for Back.
Patt 72(82) rows.

**Shape neck**
**Next row** Patt 45(49) sts, turn and work on these sts for first
side of neck.
Dec one st at neck edge, on the next 8 rows. 37(41) sts.
Work 7 rows straight.

**Shape shoulder**
Bind off 12(13) sts at beg of next and foll alt row.
Work 1 row.
Bind off rem 13(15) sts.
With right side facing, slip center 23(27) sts onto a holder,
rejoin yarn to rem sts, patt to end.
Complete to match first side.

**SLEEVES**
Using US 3 (3¼mm) needles and C cast on 59 sts.
**1st row** K1, p2, Cr2R, k1, Cr2L, p2, ★ k3, p2, Cr2R, k1,
Cr2L, p2; rep from ★ to last st, k1.
**2nd row** P1, k2, p1, [k1, p1] twice, k2, ★ p3, k2, p1, [k1, p1]
twice, k2; rep from ★ to last st, p1.
Cont in M only. These 2 rows set the welt patt.
Work a further 16 rows, inc 2 sts evenly across row. 61 sts.
Change to US 6 (4mm) needles and patt.
**1st row** Work across last 7 sts of 1st row of panel B, k4, work
across 1st row of panel C, k4, work across first 7 sts of 1st
row of panel B.
**2nd row** Work across last 7 sts of 2nd row of panel B, p4,
work across 2nd row of panel C, p4, work across first 7 sts of
2nd row of panel B.
**3rd row** Work across last 7 sts of 3rd row of panel B, C4F,
work across 3rd row of panel C, C4B, work across first 7 sts
3rd row of panel B.
**4th row** Work across last 7 sts of 4th row of panel B, p4,
work across 4th row of panel C, p4, work across first 7 sts of
4th row of panel B.
These 4 rows form cable panels and set the patt for panels A,
and B.
Cont in patt **at the same** time inc and work into patt one st
at each end of the next and every foll 4th row until there are
85(91) sts, working inc sts into panel B and 4 st cable panel,
and rem sts in reversed st st.
Cont straight until sleeve measures 10(11¾)in/25(30)cm from
cast on edge, ending with a wrong side row.
Bind off.

## NECKBAND

Join right shoulder seam.

With US 3 (3¼mm) needles, right side facing and M, pick up and k18(19) sts down left front neck, k23(27) sts from center front holder, pick up and k17(18) sts up right side of front neck, 7(8) sts down right side of back neck, k27(31) sts from back neck holder, 7(8) sts up left side of back neck. 99(111) sts.

**Next row** P3, ★ k4, p1, k4, p3; rep from ★ to end.

Starting with 1st row work 16 rows in welt patt as given for Back.

Change to C.

Work 2 rows in patt

Bind off loosely in patt.

## POCKET TOP

With US 3 (3¼mm) needles, right side facing and C, bind off sts in patt.

## FINISH

Join left shoulder and neckband. Sew on sleeves. Sew pocket lining in place. Join side and sleeve seams.

# BUTTERFLY cardigan

This pretty, summer cardigan with butterfly motifs has a contrasting checked border and rolled edge. The butterfly theme is carried through on the small bag with beads on page 38.

**Materials**

9(10) 50g balls of Debbie Bliss cotton double knitting in Pale Blue (M). One ball each of Red (A), Mid Blue (B) and Navy (C). Pair each of US 5 (3¾mm) and US 6 (4mm) knitting needles. 7 buttons.

**Measurements**

| To fit ages | 2 | 3 | years. |
|---|---|---|---|
| *Actual measurements* | | | |
| Chest | 29 | 30¾ | in |
| | 74 | 78 | cm |
| Length to shoulder | 13 | 13¾ | in |
| | 33 | 35 | cm |
| Sleeve length | 8¼ | 9½ | in |
| | 21 | 24 | cm |

**Gauge**

20 sts and 28 rows to 4in/10cm square over st st using US 6 (4mm) needles.

**Abbreviations**

See page 127.

**Note**

Read chart from right to left on right side rows and from left to right on wrong side rows (see page 113). When working motifs, use separate balls of yarn for each area of color and twist yarns together on wrong side to avoid holes (see page 116).

## BACK

With US 6 (4mm) needles and A, cast on 76(80) sts.
Beg with a k row, work 3 rows in st st.
**4th row** P ★ 2B, 2C; rep from ★ to end.
**5th row** K ★ 2C, 2B; rep from ★ to end.
**6th row** P ★ 2M, 2B; rep from ★ to end.
**7th row** K ★ 2B, 2M; rep from ★ to end.
Beg with a p row, work 3(5) rows st st in M.
Work in st st and patt from Chart 1 until row 44(42) has been worked.

### Shape armholes

Bind off 3(4) sts at beg of next 2 rows.
70(72) sts.
Cont straight until row 84(88) has been worked.
Cont in M only.

### Shape shoulders

Bind off 10(11) sts at the beg of the next 2 rows and 10 sts at beg of foll 2 rows.
Bind off rem 30 sts.

## LEFT FRONT

With US 6 (4mm) needles and A, cast on 37(39) sts.
Beg with a k row, work 3 rows in st st.
**4th row** P1(3)B, ★ 2C, 2B; rep from ★ to end.
**5th row** K ★ 2B, 2C; rep from ★ to last 1(3) sts, 1(3)B.
**6th row** P1(3)M, ★ 2B, 2M; rep from ★ to end.
**7th row** K ★ 2M, 2B; rep from ★ to last 1(3) sts, 1(3)M.
Beg with a p row, work 3(5) rows st st in M.
Work in st st and patt from Chart 1 until row 44(42) has been worked.

## Shape armhole

Bind off 3(4) sts at beg of next row. 34(35) sts.
Cont in st st and patt from Chart 1 until row
57(60) has been worked.

## Shape front

Dec one st at front edge on next 4 rows and
every foll alt row until 20(21) sts rem.
Cont straight until row 84(88) of Chart 1 has
been worked.
Cont in M only.

## Shape shoulder

Bind off 10 (11) sts at the beg of the next row.
Work 1 row.
Bind off rem 10 sts.

## RIGHT FRONT

With US 6 (4mm) needles and A, cast on
37(39) sts.
Beg with a k row, work 3 rows in st st.
4th row P ★ 2C, 2B; rep from ★ to last 1(3)
sts, 1(3)C.
5th row K1(3)C, ★ 2B, 2C; rep from ★ to end.
6th row P ★ 2B, 2M; rep from ★ to last 1(3)
sts, 1(3)B.
7th row K1(3)B, ★ 2M, 2B; rep from ★ to
end.
Beg with a p row, work 3(5) rows st st in M.
Work in st st and patt from Chart 1 until row
45(43) has been worked.

## Shape armhole

Bind off 3(4) sts at beg of next row. 34(35) sts.
Cont in st st and patt from Chart 1 until row
57(60) has been worked.

## Shape front

Dec one st at front edge on next 4 rows and
every foll alt row until 20(21) sts rem.
Cont straight until row 84(88) of Chart 1 has
been worked.
Cont in M only.
Work 1 row.

## Shape shoulder

Bind off 10 (11) sts at the beg of the next row.
Work 1 row.
Bind off rem 10 sts.

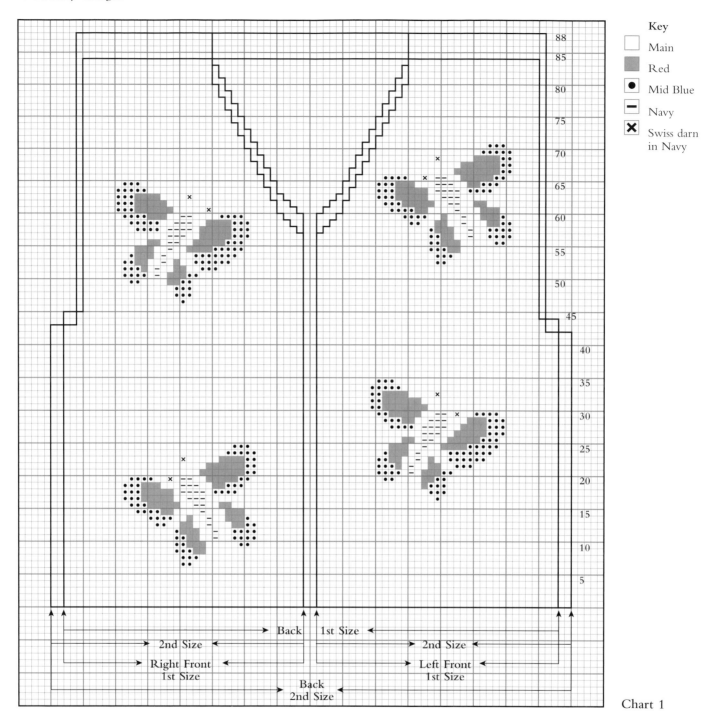

Chart 1

**Key**

| | |
|---|---|
| ☐ | Main |
| ▦ | Red |
| ● | Mid Blue |
| — | Navy |
| ✕ | Swiss darn in Navy |

**SLEEVES**

With US 6 (4mm) needles and A, cast on 36(40) sts.

Beg with a k row, work 3 rows in st st.

**4th row** P ★ 2B, 2C; rep from ★ to end.

**5th row** K ★ 2C, 2B; rep from ★ to end.

**6th row** P ★ 2M, 2B; rep from ★ to end.

**7th row** K ★ 2B, 2M; rep from ★ to end.

Beg with a p row, work 1(5) rows st st in M.

Cont in patt from Chart 2 **at the same time** inc one st at each end of the 6th and every

foll 5th row until there are 56(62) sts.

Cont straight until row 62(66) of Chart 2 has been worked.

Bind off.

**FRONTBAND**

Join shoulder seams.

With right side facing, using US 5 (3¾mm) needles and M, pick up and k51(55) sts along left front to beg of neck shaping, 18(20) sts to shoulder, 30 sts across back neck, 18(20) sts to beg of neck shaping and 51(55) sts along right front. 168(180) sts.

Chart 2

P 1 row.

**1st row** K ★ 2M, 2B; rep from ★ to end.
**2nd row** P ★ 2B, 2M; rep from ★ to end.
**3rd row** (Buttonhole row) K2B, (yf, k2togC, k2B, k2C, k2B] 6 times, yf, k2togC, ★k2B, k2C; rep from ★ to end.
**4th row** P ★ 2C, 2B; rep from ★ to end.
Change to A.
Beg with a k row, work 3 rows in st st.
Bind off.

**FINISH**
Sew on sleeves, sewing last 4(6) rows to sts bind off underarm, placing center of sleeves to shoulder seams. Join side and sleeve seams. Sew on buttons. Swiss darn butterfly antenna in C as shown on Chart.

# SNOWFLAKE AND heart baby throw

For a soft throw for a winter baby, cotton is great next to the skin. The snowflake and heart motifs are inspired by a Nordic theme and worked in a cool cream and pale blue. The hearts are decorated with simple embroidery.

**Materials**

Eight 50g balls of Debbie Bliss cotton double knitting in Main Color (M). Two balls in Contrast Color (C). Pair of US 6 (4mm) knitting needles.

**Measurements**

Approximately 24in x 29½in/61cm x 75cm.

**Gauge**

20 sts and 28 rows to 4in/10cm square over st st using US 6 (4mm) needles.

**Abbreviations**

See page 127.

**Note**

Read chart from right to left on right side rows and from left to right on wrong side rows (see page 113). When working motifs, use separate balls of yarn for each area of color and twist yarns together on wrong side to avoid holes (see page 116). Embroidery for Motif C (see page 122).

**TO MAKE**

Using M, cast on 128 sts.

K 5 rows.

Cont in patt as folls:

**1st row** K2, patt across 1st row of Motif A, k2, patt across 1st row of Motif B, k2, patt across 1st row of Motif C, k2, patt across 1st row of Motif B, k2, patt across 1st row of Motif D, k2, patt across 1st row of Motif B, k2.

**2nd row** K2, patt across 2nd row of Motif B, k2, patt across 2nd row of Motif D, k2, patt across 2nd row of Motif B, k2, patt across 2nd row of Motif C, k2, patt across 2nd row of Motif B, k2, patt across 2nd row of Motif A, k2.

These 2 rows set the patt.

Cont in patt until 24 rows of motifs have been worked.

**25th to 28th rows** K to end.

**29th row** K2, patt across 1st row of Motif B, k2, patt across 1st row of Motif C, k2, patt across 1st row of Motif B, k2, patt across 1st row of Motif D, k2, patt across 1st row of Motif B, k2, patt across 1st row of Motif A, k2.

**30th row** K2, patt across 2nd row of Motif A, k2, patt across 2nd row of Motif B, k2, patt across 2nd row of Motif D, k2, patt across 2nd row of Motif B, k2, patt across 2nd row of Motif C, k2, patt across 2nd row of Motif B, k2.

These 2 rows set the patt.

Cont in patt until 24 rows of motifs have been worked.

**53rd to 56th rows** K to end.

**57th row** K2, patt across 1st row of Motif C, k2, patt across 1st row of Motif B, k2, patt across 1st row of Motif D, k2, patt across 1st row of Motif B, k2, patt across 1st row of Motif A, k2, patt across 1st row of Motif B, k2.

**58th row** K2, patt across 2nd row of Motif B, k2, patt across 2nd row of Motif A, k2, patt across 2nd row of Motif B, k2, patt across 2nd row of Motif D, k2, patt across 2nd row of Motif B, k2, patt across 2nd row of Motif C, k2.

These 2 rows set the patt.

Cont in patt until 24 rows of motifs have been worked.

**81st to 84th rows** K to end.

**85th row** K2, patt across 1st row of Motif B, k2, patt across 1st row of Motif D, k2, patt across 1st row of Motif B, k2, patt across 1st row of Motif A, k2, patt across 1st row of Motif B, k2, patt across 1st row of Motif C, k2.

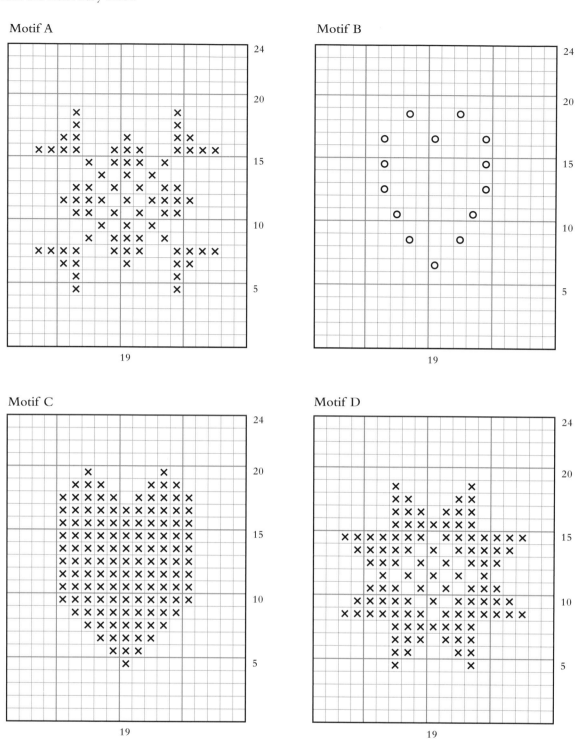

**Motif A**

**Motif B**

**Motif C**

**Motif D**

**Key**

Main

Contrast

Mb – Using M, k into front, back and front of next st, turn, p3, turn, sl1, k2 tog, psso

1st row of Motif A, k2, patt across 1st row of Motif B, k2, patt across 1st row of Motif C, k2, patt across 1st row of Motif B, k2, patt across 1st row of Motif D, k2.

**142nd row** K2, patt across 2nd row of Motif D, k2, patt across 2nd row of Motif B, k2, patt across 2nd row of Motif C, k2, patt across 2nd row of Motif B, k2, patt across 2nd row of Motif A, k2, patt across row 2 of Motif B, k2.

These 2 rows set the patt.

Cont in patt until 24 rows of motifs have been worked.

**165th to 168th rows** K to end.

**169th to 220th rows** As 1st to 52nd rows.

**221st to 226th rows** K to end.

Bind off.

**TO COMPLETE**

Using M, work 5 lazy daisy stitches on each heart on Motif C (see page 122). Using C, make 4 pom-poms and sew one to each corner.

**86th row** K2, patt across 2nd row of Motif C, k2, patt across 2nd row of Motif B, k2, patt across 2nd row of Motif A, k2, patt across 2nd row of Motif B, k2, patt across 2nd row of Motif D, k2, patt across 2nd row of Motif B, k2.

These 2 rows set the patt.

Cont in patt until 24 rows of motifs have been worked.

**109th to 112nd rows** K to end.

**113th row** K2, patt across 1st row of Motif D, k2, patt across 1st row of Motif B, k2, patt across 1st row of Motif A, k2, patt across 1st row of Motif B, k2, patt across 1st row of Motif C, k2, patt across 1st row of Motif B, k2.

**114th row** K2, patt across 2nd row of Motif B, k2, patt across 2nd row of Motif C, k2, patt across 2nd row of Motif B, k2, patt across 2nd row of Motif A, k2, patt across 2nd row of Motif B, k2, patt across 2nd row of Motif D, k2.

These 2 rows set the patt.

Cont in patt until 24 rows of motifs have been worked.

**137th to 140th rows** K to end.

**141st row** K2, patt across 1st row of Motif B, k2, patt across

# RAGLAN SWEATER with collar

This design has raglan shaping with cable detailing and cuffs that echo the split collar. It can be worn as a cropped, body-hugging sweater by knitting it in a smaller size than you would normally work.

## MATERIALS

10(11:12) 50g balls of Debbie Bliss cotton double knitting. Pair each of US 3 (3¼mm) and US 6 (4mm) knitting needles. Set of 4 double pointed US 6 (4mm) needles. Cable needle.

## Measurements

| To fit | 32 | 34 | 36 | in |
|---|---|---|---|---|
| | 87 | 91 | 96 | cm |
| *Actual measurements* | | | | |
| Bust | 36¼ | 39½ | 42½ | in |
| | 92 | 100 | 108 | cm |
| Length to shoulder | 19¼ | 20 | 21 | in |
| | 49 | 51 | 53 | cm |
| Sleeve length | 12½ | 13 | 13½ | in |
| (cuff turned back) | 32 | 33 | 34 | cm |

## Gauge

20 sts and 28 rows to 4in/10cm square over st st using US 6 (4mm) needles.

## Abbreviations

**C4F** – slip next 2 sts onto cable needle and leave at front, k2, then k2 from cable needle.
**C4B** – slip next 2 sts onto cable needle and leave at back, k2, then k2 from cable needle.
See pages 118 and 127.

## BACK AND FRONT (BOTH ALIKE)

With US 3 (3¼mm) needles cast on 82(90:98) sts.
**1st row** K2, ★ p2, k2; rep from ★ to end.
**2nd row** P2, ★ k2, p2; rep from ★ to end.
Rep the last 2 rows for 3½in/9cm, ending with a 2nd row.
Change to US 6 (4mm) needles.
Beg with a k row, cont in st st.
Work 8(10:10) rows in st st.
**Inc row** K3, m1, k to last 3 sts, m1, k3.
Inc one st at each end of row, as set, on every foll 6th row until there are 94(102:110) sts.
Cont straight until back measures 9¾ (10¼:10½)in/25(26:27)cm from cast on edge, ending with a p row.

**Shape raglan armholes**

Bind off 3(5:7) sts at beg of next 2 rows.

**1st row** K2, p1, k4, p1, k1, skpo, k to last 11 sts, k2 **tog, k1, p1, k4, p1, k2.**

**2nd row** P to end.

**3rd row** As 1st row.

**4th row** As 2nd row.

**5th row** K2, p1, C4F, p1, k1, skpo, k to last 11 sts, k2 tog, k1, p1, C4B, p1, k2.

**6th row** P to end.

Rep the last 6 rows until 32(34:36) sts rem, ending with a right side row.

**Next row** P2 tog, p2, p2 tog, p to last 6 sts, p2 tog, p2, p2 tog. 28(30:32) sts.

Leave these sts on a holder.

**SLEEVES**

**First half of cuff**

With US 3 (3¼mm) needles cast on 25(27:29) sts.

**1st row** K3, ★ p2, k2; rep from ★ to last 2(0:2) sts, p2(0:2).

**2nd row** K2(0:2), ★ p2, k2; rep from ★ to last 3 sts, p2, k1.

Rep the last 2 rows for 1½in/4cm, ending row with a 2nd row.

Leave these sts on a spare needle.

## 2nd half of cuff

With US 3 (3¼mm) needles cast on 25(27:29) sts.

**1st row** P2(0:2), ★ k2, p2; rep from ★ to last 3 sts, k3.

**2nd row** K1, p2, ★ k2, p2; rep from ★ to last 2(0:2) sts, k2(0:2).

Rep the last 2 rows for 1½in/4cm, ending with a 2nd row.

**Next row** P2(0:2), ★ k2, p2; rep from ★ to last 3 sts, k2, p1, then work across sts of 1st half of cuff as folls: p1, k2, ★ p2, k2; rep from ★ to last 2(0:2) sts, p2(0:2). 50(54:58) sts.

Cont in rib as set until cuff measures 5½in/14cm from cast on edge, ending with a 2nd row, inc one st at center. 51(55:59) sts.

Change to US 6 (4mm) needles.

Beg with a k row, work 2 rows in st st.

**Inc row** K3, m1, k to last 3 sts, m1, k3.

Inc one st at each end of row, as set, on every foll 6th and 4th row alternately until there are 73(79:85) sts.

Cont straight until sleeve measures 15¼(15¾:16)in/39(40:41)cm from cast on edge, ending with a wrong side row.

## Shape raglan top

Bind off 3(5:7) sts at beg of next 2 rows.

**1st row** K2, p1, k4, p1, k1, skpo, k to last 11 sts, k2 tog, k1, p1, k4, p1, k2.

**2nd row** P to end.

**3rd row** K2, p1, k4, p1, k to last 8 sts, p1, k4, p1, k2.

**4th row** As 2nd row.

**5th row** K2, p1, C4F, p1, k1, skpo, k to last 11 sts, k2 tog, k1, p1, C4B, p1, k2.

**6th row** As 2nd row.

**7th row** K2, p1, k4, p1, k to last 8 sts, p1, k4, p1, k2.

**8th row** P to end.

**9th row** K2, p1, k4, p1, k1, skpo, k to last 11 sts, k2 tog, k1, p1, k4, p1, k2.

**10th row** As 2nd row.

**11th row** K2, p1, C4F, p1, k to last 8 sts, p1, C4B, p1, k2.

**12th row** As 2nd row.

**13th to 16th rows** As 1st to 4th rows.

Cont to work cables on next and every 6th row, **at the same time** dec as set on next and every foll alt row until 21 sts rem, ending with a p row.

**Next row** K2, p1, patt 4, p1, k1, sl 1, k2 tog, psso, k1, p1, patt 4, p1, k2. 19 sts.

**Next row** P2 tog, p2, p2 tog, p to last 6 sts, p2 tog, p2, p2 tog. 15 sts.

Leave these sts on a holder.

## COLLAR

Join raglan seams.

With set of four US 6 (4mm) double pointed needles and right side facing, slip first 14(15:16) sts from center front neck on to a safety pin, k rem 14(15:16) sts, k15 sts from top of sleeve, inc 2 sts evenly k across 28(30:32) sts from back neck holder, k15 sts from top of sleeve, then k14(15:16) sts from holder. 88(92:96) sts.

**1st rib round** [K1, p2, k1] to end.

Rib 19 more rounds, turn.

**1st rib row** K3, ★ p2, k2; rep from ★ to last 5 sts, p2, k3.

**2nd rib row** K1, ★ p2, k2; rep from ★ to last 3 sts, p2, k1.

Work 14 rows rib as set. Bind off in rib.

## FINISH

Join side and sleeve seams, reversing cuff on last 3in/8cm.

# RUGBY shirt

Based on the classic British rugby shirt, this design has multi-colored stripes contrasted against a crisp, white collar. Stripes are fun to knit, particularly if you want to avoid complicated color techniques.

## Materials

2(3:3) 50g balls of Debbie Bliss cotton double knitting in White (M). 2(2:3) balls each of Pale Blue, Brown, Pale Pink, two balls Mid Blue, one ball each of Navy, Red and Khaki. Pair each of US 3 (3¼mm) and US 6 (4mm) knitting needles.

## Measurements

| To fit ages | 1-2 | 2-3 | 3-4 | years. |
|---|---|---|---|---|
| *Actual measurements* | | | | |
| Chest | 27½ | 29 | 31½ | in |
| | 70 | 74 | 80 | cm |
| Length to shoulder | 14¼ | 15¾ | 17 | in |
| | 36 | 40 | 43 | cm |
| Sleeve length | 8¾ | 9½ | 11 | in |
| | 22 | 24 | 28 | cm |

## Gauge

20 sts and 28 rows to 4in/10cm square over st st using US 6 (4mm) needles.

## Abbreviations

See page 127.

Stripe patt: 3 rows Pale Blue, 3 rows Brown, 1 row White, 2 rows Olive Green, 3 rows Pale Pink, 2 rows Red, 1 row White, 4 rows Mid Blue, 1 row Navy and 1 row White.

## BACK

With US 3 (3¼mm) needles and Pale Blue, cast on 70(74:82) sts.
**1st rib row** K2, * p2, k2; rep from * to end.
**2nd rib row** P2, * k2, p2; rep from * to end.
Rep the last 2 rows once more, inc 2(2:0) sts evenly across last row. 72(76:82) sts.
Change to US 6 (4mm) needles.
Beg with a k row cont in st st and stripe patt until back measures 14¼(15¾:17)in/36(40:43)cm from cast on edge, ending with a p row.

## Shape shoulders

Bind off 12(12:13) sts at beg of next 2 rows and 11(12:13) sts on foll 2 rows.
Leave rem 26(28:30) sts on a holder.

## FRONT

Work as given for Back until front measures 10(11:12¼)in/25(28:31)cm from cast on edge, ending with a p row.

### Divide for front opening

**Next row** K34(36:39), turn and work on these sts for first side of front neck. Work 2(2¼:2¼)in/5(6:6)cm straight, ending at side edge.

### Shape neck

**Next row** K to last 6(7:8) sts, leave these sts on a safety pin.

Dec one st at neck edge on every row until 23(24:26) sts rem.

Work straight until front measures the same as Back to shoulder, ending at side edge.

### Shape shoulder

Bind off 12(12:13) sts at beg of next row.

Work 1 row. Bind off rem 11(12:13) sts.

With right side facing, join on yarn, bind off center 4 sts, k to end.

Complete to match first side of neck.

## SLEEVES

Using US 3 (3¼mm) needles and Pale Blue, cast on 38(38:42) sts.

Work 1½(2:2)in/4(5:5)cm rib as given for Back, ending with a right side row.

**Inc row** Rib 4(5:4), ★ m1, rib 6(4:7); rep from ★ to last 4(5:3) sts, m1, rib 4(5:3). 44(46:48) sts.

Change to US 6 (4mm) needles.

Beg with a k row and working in stripe patt as before, inc one st at each end of the 3rd and every foll 4th(4th:5th) row until there are 64(68:72) sts.

Cont straight until sleeve measures 8¾(9½:11)in/22(24:28)cm from cast on edge, ending with a p row.

Bind off.

## LEFT FRONT BAND

With right side facing, US 3 (3¼mm) needles and White, pick up and k16 sts down left side of front neck.

**1st row** K1, [p2, k2] 3 times, p2, k1.

**2nd row** K3, [p2, k2] twice, p2, k3.

Rep the last 2 rows once more and the 1st row again.

Bind off in rib.

## RIGHT FRONT BAND

With right side facing, US 3 (3¼mm) needles and White, pick up and k16 sts up right side of front neck.

Work 5 rows rib as given for Left Front Band.

## COLLAR

Join shoulder seams.

With right side facing, US 3 (3¼mm) needles and White, slip 6(7:8) sts from safety pin on right front neck onto a needle, pick up and k15(15:17) sts up right side of front neck, k26(28:30) sts from back neck holder, pick up and k15(15:17) sts down left side of front neck, k6(7:8) sts from safety pin on left front neck. 68(72:80) sts.

**1st row** K1, |p2, k2| 16(17:19) times, p2, k1

Cont in rib as for Left Front Band.

**Next 2 rows** Rib to last 20 sts, turn.

**Next 2 rows** Rib to last 16 sts, turn.

**Next 2 rows** Rib to last 12 sts, turn.

**Next 2 rows** Rib to last 8 sts, turn.

**Next row** Rib to last 5 sts, p2, k3.

Work a further 16 rows in rib.

Bind off.

## FINISH

Sew on sleeves. Join side and sleeve seams. Place lower edge of right front band over lower edge of left front band and sew in place.

# LACE AND BOBBLE throw

This throw uses the same stitch patterns as the Guernsey Dress on page 40 and the Lace and Bobble Bootees on page 46, so all the designs together would make a lovely gift set for a nearly-new baby. The throw is the ideal size for a buggy or small pram.

## Materials

Six 50g balls of Debbie Bliss wool/cotton. Pair of US 3 (3¼mm) knitting needles. Cable needle.

## Measurements

Approximately 23in x 26¾in/58cm x 68cm.

## Gauge

25 sts and 34 rows to 4in/10cm square over st st using US 3 (3¼mm) needles.

## Abbreviations

**Mb** – work k1, p1, k1, p1, k1, into next st, turn, p5, turn, pass 2nd, 3rd, 4th and 5th st over first and off the needle, then pass st back onto right hand needle.
**C4F** – slip next 2 sts onto cable needle and hold at front of work, k2, then k2 from cable needle. Also see pages 118 and 127.

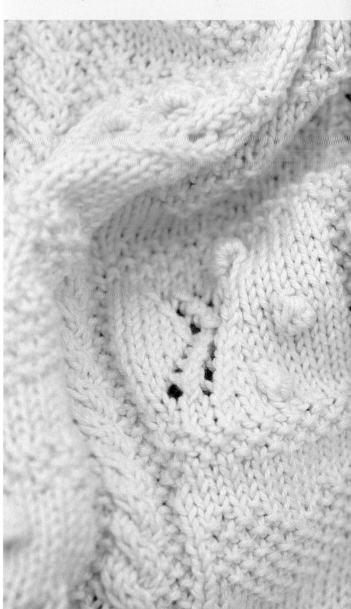

## PANEL A

(worked over 15 sts)
**1st row** K to end.
**2nd row** P to end.
**3rd row** K7, p1, k7.
**4th row** P6, k1, p1, k1, p6.
**5th row** K5, p1, [k1, p1] twice, k5.
**6th row** P4, k1, [p1, k1] 3 times, p4.
**7th row** K3, p1, [k1, p1] 4 times, k3.
**8th row** P2, k1, [p1, k1] 5 times, p2.
**9th row** K1, [p1, k1] 7 times.
**10th row** As 8th row.
**11th row** As 9th row.
**12th row** As 8th row.
**13th row** [K1, p1] 3 times, k3, [p1, k1] 3 times.
**14th row** P2, k1, p1, k1, p5, k1, p1, k1, p2.
**15th row** K to end.
**16th row** P to end.
**17th row** K to end.
**18th row** P to end.
These 18 rows form the patt panel.

## PANEL B

(worked over 15 sts)
**1st row** K to end.
**2nd and alt rows** P to end.
**3rd row** K to end.
**5th row** K6, k2 tog, yf, k7.
**7th row** K5, k2 tog, yf, k1, yf, skpo, k5.
**9th row** K4, k2 tog, yf, k3, yf, skpo, k4.
**11th row** K3, k2 tog, yf, k2, Mb, k2, yf, skpo, k3.
**13th row** K2, k2 tog, yf, k7, yf, skpo, k2.
**15th row** K1, k2 tog, yf, k2, Mb, k3, Mb, k2, yf, skpo, k1.

**17th row** K to end.
**18th row** P to end.
These 18 rows form the patt panel.

## PANEL C

(worked over 15 sts)
**1st row** K to end.
**2nd and alt rows** P to end.
**3rd row** K6, Mb, k2, [k2 tog, yf] twice, k2.
**5th row** K8, [k2 tog, yf] twice, k3.
**7th row** K7, [k2 tog, yf] twice, k4.
**9th row** K3, Mb, k2, [k2 tog, yf] twice, k5.
**11th row** K7, [yf, skpo] twice, k4.
**13th row** K8, [yf, skpo] twice, k3.
**15th row** K6, Mb, k2, [yf, skpo] twice, k2.
**17th row** K to end.
**18th row** P to end.
These 18 rows form the patt panel.

## TO MAKE

With US 3 (3¼mm) needles cast on 146 sts.
**1st row** ★ K1, [p1, k1] 10 times, C4F; rep from ★ to last 21 sts, k1, [p1, k1] 10 times.
**2nd row** ★ K1, [p1, k1] 10 times, p4; rep from ★ to last 21 sts, k1, [p1, k1] 10 times.
**3rd row** ★ K1, [p1, k1] 10 times, k4; rep from ★ to last 21 sts, k1, [p1, k1] 10 times.
**4th row** ★ K1, [p1, k1] 10 times, p4; rep from ★ to last 21 sts, k1, [p1, k1] 10 times.
These 4 rows form cable and seed st panel.
Patt 2 more rows.
**7th row** Seed st 3, work 1st row of patt panel B, patt 10, work 1st row of patt panel A, patt 10, work 1st row of patt panel C, patt 10, work 1st row of patt panel A, patt 10, work 1st row of patt panel B, patt 10, work 1st row of patt panel A, seed st 3.
**8th row** Seed st 3, work 2nd row of patt panel A, patt 10, work 2nd row of patt panel B, patt 10, work 2nd row of patt panel A, patt 10, work 2nd row of patt panel C, patt 10, work 2nd row of patt panel A, patt 10, work 2nd row of patt panel B, seed st 3.
**9th to 24th rows** Rep 7th and 8th rows eight times, working 3rd to 18th rows of patt panels.
**25th row** ★ K1, [p1, k1] 10 times, C4F; rep from ★ to last 21 sts, k1, [p1, k1] 10 times.
**26th row** ★ K1, [p1, k1] 10 times, p4; rep from ★ to last 21 sts, k1, [p1, k1] 10 times.

**27th row** ★ K1, [p1, k1] 10 times, k4; rep from ★ to last 21 sts, k1, [p1, k1] 10 times.
**28th row** ★ K1, [p1, k1] 10 times, p4; rep from ★ to last 21 sts, k1, [p1, k1] 10 times.
**29th row** Seed st 3, work 1st row of patt panel A, patt 10, work 1st row of patt panel C, patt 10, work 1st row of patt panel A, patt 10, work 1st row of patt panel B, patt 10, work 1st row of patt panel A, patt 10, work 1st row of patt panel C, seed st 3.
**30th row** Seed st 3, work 2nd row of patt panel C, patt 10, work 2nd row of patt panel A, patt 10, work 2nd row of patt panel B, patt 10, work 2nd row of patt panel A, patt 10, work 2nd row of patt panel C, patt 10, work 2nd row of patt panel A, seed st 3.
**31st to 46th rows** Rep 29th and 30th rows eight times, working 3rd to 18th rows of patt panels.
**47th row** ★ K1, [p1, k1] 10 times, k4; rep from ★ to last 21 sts, k1, [p1, k1] 10 times.
**48th row** ★ K1, [p1, k1] 10 times, p4; rep from ★ to last 21 sts, k1, [p1, k1] 10 times.
**49th row** ★ K1, [p1, k1] 10 times, C4F; rep from ★ to last 21 sts, k1, [p1, k1] 10 times.
**50th row** ★ K1, [p1, k1] 10 times, p4; rep from ★ to last 21 sts, k1, [p1, k1] 10 times.
**51st row** Seed st 3, work 1st row of patt panel C, patt 10, work 1st row of patt panel A, patt 10, work 1st row of patt panel B, patt 10, work 1st row of patt panel A, patt 10, work 1st row of patt panel C, patt 10, work 1st row of patt panel A, seed st 3.
**52nd row** Seed st 3, work 2nd row of patt panel A, patt 10, work 2nd row of patt panel C, patt 10, work 2nd row of patt panel A, patt 10, work 2nd row of patt panel B, patt 10, work 2nd row of patt panel A, patt 10, work 2nd row of patt panel C, seed st 3.
**53rd to 68th rows** Rep 51st and 52nd rows eight times, working 3rd to 18th rows of patt panels.
**69th row** ★ K1, [p1, k1] 10 times, C4F; rep from ★ to last 21 sts, k1, [p1, k1] 10 times.
**70th row** ★ K1, [p1, k1] 10 times, p4; rep from ★ to last 21 sts, k1, [p1, k1] 10 times.
**71st row** ★ K1, [p1, k1] 10 times, k4; rep from ★ to last 21 sts, k1, [p1, k1] 10 times.
**72nd row** ★ K1, [p1, k1] 10 times, p4; rep from ★ to last 21 sts, k1, [p1, k1] 10 times.
**73rd row** Seed st 3, work 1st row of patt panel A, patt 10, work 1st row of patt panel B, patt 10, work 1st row of patt panel A, patt 10, work 1st row of patt panel C, patt 10, work 1st row of patt panel A, patt 10, work 1st row of patt panel B, seed st 3.
**74th row** Seed st 3, work 2nd row of patt panel B, patt 10,

work 2nd row of patt panel A, patt 10, work 2nd row of patt panel C, patt 10, work 2nd row of patt panel A, patt 10, work 2nd row of patt panel B, patt 10, work 2nd row of patt panel A, seed st 3.

**75th to 90th rows** Rep 73rd and 74th rows eight times, working 3rd to 18th rows of patt panels.

**91st row** ★ K1, [p1, k1] 10 times, k4; rep from ★ to last 21 sts, k1, [p1, k1] 10 times.

**92nd row** ★ K1, [p1, k1] 10 times, p4; rep from ★ to last 21 sts, k1, [p1, k1] 10 times.

**93rd row** ★ K1, [p1, k1] 10 times, C4F; rep from ★ to last 21 sts, k1, [p1, k1] 10 times.

**94th row** ★ K1, [p1, k1] 10 times, p4; rep from ★ to last 21 sts, k1, [p1, k1] 10 times.

**95th to 182nd rows** Work as given for 7th to 94th rows.

**183rd to 248th rows** Work as given for 7th to 72nd rows.

**249th row** ★ K1, [p1, k1] 10 times, C4F; rep from ★ to last 21 sts, k1, [p1, k1] 10 times.

**250th row** ★ K1, [p1, k1] 10 times, p4; rep from ★ to last 21 sts, k1, [p1, k1] 10 times.
Bind off.

# STRIPED sweater

A simple top with stripes that has a square, nautical-style neckline and neat side vents. The buttoned shoulder fastening makes it easy to pull on and off over a small child's head. It is a perfect design for the fairly new knitter.

## Materials
3(4:5:6) 50g balls of Debbie Bliss wool/cotton in White (M). 1(1:2:2) balls in Aqua (C). Pair each of US 2 (2¾mm) and US 3 (3¼mm) knitting needles. 2 buttons.

## Measurements

| To fit ages | 6-12 | 12-18 | 18-24 | 24-36 | months. |
|---|---|---|---|---|---|
| *Actual measurements* | | | | | |
| Chest | 22 | 24½ | 26¾ | 29 | in |
| | 56 | 62 | 68 | 74 | cm |
| Length to shoulder | 11 | 12¼ | 13½ | 15 | in |
| | 28 | 31 | 34 | 38 | cm |
| Sleeve length | 6¼ | 7 | 8¼ | 9½ | in |
| | 16 | 18 | 21 | 24 | cm |

## Gauge
25 sts and 34 rows to 4in/10cm square over st st using US 3 (3¼mm) needles.

## Abbreviations
See page 127.

## BACK
With US 2 (2¾mm) needles and M, cast on 72(80:86:94) sts.
K 7 rows to form garter st hem.
Change to US 3 (3¼mm) needles.
**1st row** With M, k to end.
**2nd row** With M, k3, p to last 3 sts, k3.
**3rd row** With M, k to end.
**4th row** With M, k3, p to last 3 sts, k3.
**5th row** With M, k3, with C, k to last 3 sts, with M, k3.
**6th row** With M, k3, with C, p to last 3 sts, with M, k3.
Beg with a k row work in st st across all sts and stripe patt of [2 rows M, 2 rows C] twice, 4 rows M and 2 rows C until 42(42:56:56) rows have been worked in striped patt from top of garter st hem.
Cont in st st and M only until back measures 9½(10¾:11¾:13½)in/24(27:30:34)cm from cast on edge, ending with a wrong side row.

### Shape shoulders and back neck
**Next row** K21(24:27:30) sts, turn and work on this set of sts only.
Cont straight until back measures 10¾(12:13:14¾)in/27(30:33:37)cm from cast

on edge, ending with a wrong side row.
Change to US 2 (2¾mm) needles.
With M, k 3 rows.
Bind off.
With right side facing, slip center
30(32:32:34) sts onto a holder, join on yarn,
patt to end.
Cont straight until back measures
10¾(12:13:14¾)in/27(30:33:37)cm from cast
on edge, ending with a wrong side row.
Change to US 2 (2¾mm) needles.
With M, k 5 rows.
Bind off.

## FRONT

Work as given for Back until front measures
8¾(10:11¼:12¼)in/22(25:28:31)cm from cast
on edge, ending with a wrong side row.

### Shape shoulders and front neck

**Next row** K21(24:27:30) sts, turn and work
on this set of sts only.
Cont straight until front measures same as
Back to shoulder, ending with a wrong side row.

### Shape shoulder

Change to US 2 (2¾mm) needles.
K 2 rows

**Buttonhole row** K14(16:18:20), k2tog, yf, k to end.
K 2 rows.
Bind off.
With right side facing, slip center 30(32:32:34) sts onto a
holder, join on yarn, k to end.
Cont straight until front measures same as Back to shoulder,
ending with a wrong side row.
Change to US 2 (2¾mm) needles.
With M, k 3 rows.
Bind off.

## SLEEVES

With US 2 (2¾mm) needles and M, cast on 46(46:50:50) sts.
**1st row** K2, ★ p2, k2; rep from ★ to end.
**2nd row** P2, ★ k2, p2; rep from ★ to end.
Rep the last 2 rows for ¾(¾:1¼:1¼)in/2(2:3:3)cm, ending
with a 2nd row.
Change to US 3 (3¼mm) needles.
Beg with a k row, cont in st st and stripe sequence of 4 rows
M, [2 rows C, 2 rows M] twice, and 2 rows C, **at the same
time** inc one st at each end of the 3rd and every foll 4th row
until there are 62(68:74:78) sts.
Cont straight until sleeve measures 6¼(7:8¼:9½)in/
16(18:21:24)cm.
Bind off.

## BACK NECKBAND

With US 2 (2¾mm) needles M and right side facing, pick up and k7 sts down right side of back neck, k30(32:32:34) sts from back neck, pick up and k9 sts up left side of back neck. 46(48:48:50) sts. K 1 row.

**Dec row** K5, skpo, k2 tog, k26(28:28:30), skpo, k2 tog, k7. K 1 row.

**Dec row** K4, skpo, k2 tog, k24(26:26:28), skpo, k2 tog, k6. K 1 row. Bind off, dec as before.

## FRONT NECKBAND

With US 2 (2¾mm) needles M and right side facing, pick up and k14 sts down left side of front neck, k30(32:32:34) sts from front neck, pick up and k12 sts up right side of front neck. 56(58:58:60) sts. K 1 row.

**Dec row** K2, k2 tog, yf, k8, skpo, k2 tog, k26(28:28:30), skpo, k2 tog, k10. K 1 row.

**Dec row** K11, skpo, k2 tog, k24(26:26:30), skpo, k2 tog, k9. K 1 row. Bind off, dec as before.

## FINISH

Join right shoulder seam. Lap left front buttonhole band over left back button band and catch side edges together. Sew on sleeves. Join side and sleeve seams to top of side slit. Sew on buttons.

# BEADED bag

This bag, with its bold blocks of color, has beads that are knitted in as you work the red windowpane check. The intarsia technique used makes this a design for the more experienced knitter.

**TO MAKE**

**First side**

With US 3 (3¼mm) needles and M cast on 67 sts.

Beg with a k row, cont in st st.

Work 2 rows.

Cont in patt from chart.

**1st row** K1A, [5A, 3B, 5A, 5M, 3B, 5M] twice, 5A, 3B, 6A.

Cont to 54th row, then work 1st to 26th rows again.

Cont in M only.

K 3 rows to form hemline.

Beg with a p row, work 11 rows in st st.

Bind off.

**Materials**

Two 50g balls of Debbie Bliss wool/cotton in Main Color (M). One ball each of Khaki (A), Red (B) and Turquoise (C). Pair of US 3 (3¼mm) needles. Two double pointed US 3 (3¼mm) needles. 432 medium purple beads.

**Measurements**

9¾in x 9in/25cm x 23cm.

**Gauge**

25 sts and 34 rows to 4in/10cm square over st st using US 3 (3¼mm) needles.

**Abbreviations**

See page 127.

**Note**

Read chart from right to left on right side rows and from left to right on wrong side rows (see page 113). Use separate balls of yarn for each area of color and twist yarns together on wrong side to avoid holes (see page 116).

Cut B into 10 lengths approximately 177in/450cm long and thread 24 beads onto each length for vertical bars and 6 lengths approximately 200in/508cm long and thread 32 beads onto each length for horizontal bars. To place a bead on right side rows, yarn to front of work, push bead up close to front of knitting, slip next stitch purlwise onto right hand needle, then yarn to back of work, leaving bead in front of slipped stitch. On wrong side rows, yarn to back of work, push bead up close to back of knitting, slip next stitch purlwise onto right hand needle, then yarn to front of work, leaving bead in front of slipped stitch. (See page 120).

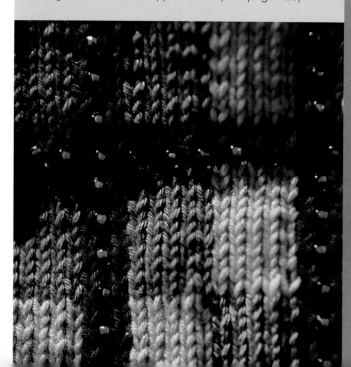

**Key**

☐ Main color (M)

● Red (B)

◎ Turquoise (C)

◤ Khaki (A)

☒ Bead placed on wrong side row

◼ Bead placed on right side row

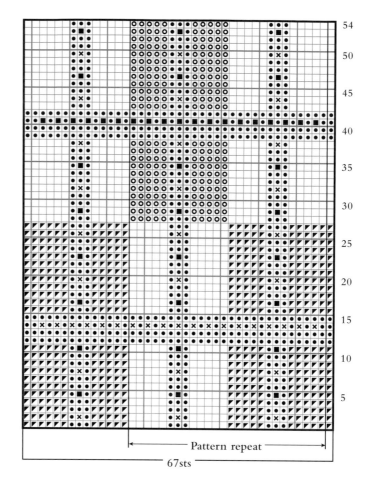

Pattern repeat

67sts

**Second side**

With right side facing US 3 (3¼mm) needles and M pick up and k67 sts along cast on edge of first side.

Beg with a p row, cont in st st.

Work 1 row.

Cont in patt from chart but using M instead of A, and A instead of M as folls:

**1st row** K1M, [5M, 3B, 5M, 5A, 3B, 5A] twice, 5M, 3B, 6M.

Cont to 54th row, then work 1st to 26th rows again.

Cont in M only.

K 3 rows to form hemline.

Beg with a p row, work 11 rows in st st.

Bind off.

**HANDLES (MAKE 2)**

With US 3 (3¼mm) double pointed needles and M cast on 6 sts.

Beg with a k row, work 10 rows st st.

**Next row** K6, do not turn, bring the yarn across the back of the work into the position to k the foll row. Cont working in this way with right side facing until handle measures 11¾in/30cm from cast on edge. With right side facing and beg with a k row work 10 rows st st.

Bind off.

**FINISH**

Join side seams, Fold facing to wrong side along hemline and sew in place.

For a firmer handle, lightly stuff through the middle of the knitted cord and secure by over sewing at both ends. Stitch in place on inside edge of hem.

# TEXTURED CARDIGAN with picot edge

This cabled cardigan is shaped to skim the body. For a less close-fitting look, you can always knit a larger size. The design is edged with a pretty picot bind off and has buttonholes concealed in the cabled front opening.

## PATT PANEL

(worked over 23(23:25) sts)

**1st row (right side)** P7(7:8), Tw4Rb, k1b, Tw4Lb, p7(7:8).

**2nd row** K7(7:8), p1, [k1, p1] 4 times, k7(7:8).

**3rd row** P6(6:7), Tw4Rb, k1, k1b, k1, Tw4Lb, p6(6:7).

**4th row** K6(6:7), p1, k1, p1, [k2, p1] twice, k1, p1, k6(6:7).

**5th row** P5(6:6), Tw4Rb, k2, k1b, k2, Tw4Lb, p5(5:6).

**6th row** K5(5:6), p1, k1, p2, k2, p1, k2, p2, k1, p1, k5(5:6).

**7th row** P4(4:5), Tw4Rb, k1b, [k2, k1b] twice, Tw4Lb, p4(4:5).

**8th row** K4(4:5), p1, [k1, p1] twice, [k2, p1] twice, [k1, p1] twice, k4(4:5).

**9th row** P3(3:4), Tw4Rb, k1, k1b, [k2, k1b] twice, k1, Tw4Lb, p3(3:4).

**10th row** K3(3:4), p1, k1, p1, [k2, p1] 4 times, k1, p1, k3(3:4).

**11th row** P2(2:3), Tw4Rb, k2, [k1b, k2] 3 times, Tw4Lb, p2(2:3).

**12th row** K2(2:3), p1, k1, p1, k3, p1, [k2, p1] twice, k3, p1, k1, p1, k2(2:3).

**13th row** P2(2:3), k1b, p1, k1b, k3, Mb, [k2, Mb] twice, k3, k1b, p1, k1b, p2(2:3).

**14th row** K2(2:3), p1, k1, p1, k3, p1b, [k2, p1b] twice, k3, p1, k1, p1, k2(2:3).

**15th row** P2(2:3), k1b, p1, k1b, p3, k1b, p1, [k1b] 3 times, p1, k1b, p3, k1b, p1, k1b, p2(2:3).

## Materials

16(17:18) 50g balls of Debbie Bliss wool/cotton. Pair each of US 2 (2¾mm) and US 3 (3¼mm) knitting needles. Cable needle. 6 buttons.

## Measurements

| To fit | | 32-34 | 36-38 | 40-42 | in |
|---|---|---|---|---|---|
| | | 81-86 | 91-97 | 102-107 | cm |

*Actual measurements*

| Bust | | 37¾ | 41 | 43¼ | in |
|---|---|---|---|---|---|
| | | 96 | 104 | 110 | cm |
| Length to shoulder | | 22 | 22¾ | 23½ | in |
| | | 56 | 58 | 60 | cm |
| Sleeve length | | 17 | 17¼ | 17¾ | in |
| | | 43 | 44 | 45 | cm |

## Gauge

25 sts and 34 rows to 4in/10cm square over st st using US 3 (3¼mm) needles.

## Abbreviations

**Tw4Rb** – slip next st onto cable needle and leave at back, k1b, p1, k1b, then p1 from cable needle.

**Tw4Lb** – slip next 3 sts onto cable needle and leave at front, p1, then k1b, p1, k1b, from cable needle.

**Mb** – work k1, p1, k1, p1, k1, into next st, turn, p5, turn, k5, pass 2nd, 3rd, 4th and 5th st over first and off the needle.

**C4F** – slip next 2 sts onto cable needle and leave at front, k2, then k2, from cable needle.

See also pages 118 and 127.

**16th row** K8(8:9), p1, k1, p3, k1, p1, k8(8:9).
These 16 rows form the patt and are
rep throughout.

**BACK**

With US 3 (3¼mm) needles cast on
152(162:170) sts.
**1st row** K12(14:14), ★ work across 1st row of
patt panel, k12(14:14); rep from ★ to end.
**2nd row** K4(5:5), p4, k4(5:5), ★ work across
2nd row of patt panel, k4(5:5), p4, k4(5:5); rep
from ★ to end.

**3rd row** K4(5:5), C4F, k4(5:5), ★ work across 3rd row of patt
panel, k4(5:5), C4F, k4(5:5); rep from ★ to end.
**4th row** K4(5:5), p4, k4(5:5), ★ work across 4th row of patt
panel, k4(5:5), p4, k4(5:5); rep from ★ to end.
These 4 rows set the position for patt panels and form garter
st and cable panels.
Cont in patt until back measures 4in/10cm from cast on
edge, ending with a 4th row of cable panel.
**1st dec row** K2(3:3), skpo, k4, k2 tog, k2(3:3), ★ work across
patt panel, k2(3:3), skpo, k4, k2 tog, k2(3:3); rep from ★ to end.
Cont in patt until back measures 6¼in/16cm from cast on
edge, ending with a 4th row of cable panel.

**2nd dec row** K1(2:2), skpo, k4, k2 tog, k1(2:2), ★ work across patt panel, k1(2:2), skpo, k4, k2 tog, k1(2:2); rep from ★ to end.

Change to US 2 (2¾mm) needles.

Cont in patt until back measures 10¼in/26cm from cast on edge, ending with a 4th row of cable panel.

Change to US 3 (3¼mm) needles.

**1st inc row** K2(3:3), m1, k4, m1, k2(3:3), ★ work across patt panel, k2(3:3), m1, k4, m1, k2(3:3); rep from ★ to end.

Cont in patt until back measures 12½in/32cm from cast on edge, ending with a 4th row of cable panel.

**2nd inc row** K3(4:4), m1, k4, m1, k3(4:4), ★ work across patt panel, k3(4:4), m1, k4, m1, k3(4:4); rep from ★ to end. 152(162:170) sts.

Cont in patt until back measures 15(15¼:15¾)in/ 38(39:40)cm from cast on edge, ending with a 4th row of cable panel.

### Shape armholes

Bind off 5 sts at beg of next 2 rows.

Dec one st at each end of next and 6(8:8) foll alt rows. 128(134:142) sts.

Cont in patt until back measures 21¼(22:22¾)in/54(56:58)cm from cast on edge, ending with a wrong side row.

### Shape neck

**Next row** Patt 50(52:55), turn and work on these sts for first side of neck.

Dec one st at neck edge on next 4 rows. 46(48:51) sts.

Work 1 row.

### Shape shoulders

Bind off 15(16:17) sts at beg of next and foll alt row.

Work 1 row.

Bind off 16(16:17) sts.

With right side facing rejoin yarn to rem sts, bind off center 28(30:32) sts, patt to end.

Complete to match first side of neck.

**LEFT FRONT**

With US 3 (3¼mm) needles cast on 80(85:89) sts.

**1st row** ★ K12(14:14), work across 1st row of patt panel; rep from ★ once more, k10(11:11).

**2nd row** K2, p4, k4(5:5), ★ work across 2nd row of patt panel, k4(5:5), p4, k4(5:5); rep from ★ once more.

**3rd row** ★ K4(5:5), C4F, k4(5:5), work across 3rd row of patt panel; rep from ★ once more, k4(5:5), C4F, k2.

**4th row** K2, p4, k4(5:5), ★ work across 4th row of patt panel, k4(5:5), p4, k4(5:5); rep from ★ once more.

These 4 rows set the position for patt panels and form garter st and cable panels.

Cont in patt until front measures 4in/10cm from cast on edge, ending with a 4th row of cable panel.

**1st dec row** ★ K2(3:3), skpo, k4, k2 tog, k2(3:3), work across patt panel; rep from ★ once more, k2(3:3), skpo, k6.

Cont in patt until front measures 6¼in/16cm from cast on edge, ending with a 4th row of cable panel.

**2nd dec row** ★ K1(2:2), skpo, k4, k2 tog, k1(2:2), work across patt panel; rep from ★ once more, k1(2:2), skpo, k6.

Change to US 2 (2¾mm) needles.

Cont in patt until front measures 10¼in/26cm from cast on edge, ending with a 4th row of cable panel.

Change to US 3 (3¼mm) needles.

**1st inc row** ★ K2(3:3), m1, k4, m1, k2(3:3), work across patt panel; rep from ★ once more, k2(3:3), m1, k6.

Cont in patt until front measures 12½in/32cm from cast on edge, ending with a 4th row of cable panel.

**2nd inc row** ★ K3(4:4), m1, k4, m1, k3(4:4), work across patt panel; rep from ★ once more, k3(4:4), m1, k6. 80(85:89) sts.

Cont in patt until front measures 15(15¼:15¾)in/38(39:40)cm from cast on edge, ending with a 4th row of cable panel.

**Shape armhole and front neck**
Bind off 5 sts at beg of next row.
Patt 1 row.
**1st row** Skpo, patt to last 8 sts, k2 tog, patt 4, k2.
**2nd row** Patt to end.
**3rd row** Skpo, patt to last 6 sts, patt 4, k2.
**4th row** Patt 1 row.
Rep the last 4 rows 2(3:3) times more, then the first row again.
Keeping armhole edge straight cont to dec at neck edge on every 4th row until 46(48:51) sts rem.
Work straight until front matches Back to shoulders, ending at armhole edge.

**Shape shoulder**
Bind off 15(16:17) sts at beg of next and foll alt row.
Patt 1 row.
Bind off rem 16(16:17) sts.
Mark position of buttons, the first 4in/10cm from cast on edge, the sixth ¾in/2cm below neck shaping, the rem 4 spaced evenly between.

**RIGHT FRONT**
With US 3 (3¼mm) needles cast on 80(85:89) sts.
**1st row** K10(11:11), ★ work across 1st row of patt panel, k12(14:14); rep from ★ once more.
**2nd row** ★K4(5:5), p4, k4(5:5), work across 2nd row of patt panel; rep from ★ once more, k4(5:5), p4, k2.
**3rd row** K2, C4F, k4(5:5), ★ work across 3rd row of patt panel, k4(5:5), C4F, k4(5:5); rep from ★ once more.
**4th row** ★ K4(5:5), p4, k4(5:5), ★ work across 4th row of patt panel; rep from ★ once more, k4(5:5), p4, k2.
These 4 rows set the position for patt panels and form garter st and cable panels.
Cont in patt until front measures 4in/10cm from cast on edge, ending with a 4th row of cable panel.
**1st dec and buttonhole row** K3, skpo, yf, k1, k2 tog, k2(3:3), ★ work across patt panel, k2(3:3), skpo, k4, k2 tog, k2(3:3); rep from ★ once more.
Cont in patt, working buttonholes to match

markers, until front measures 6¼in/16cm from cast on edge, ending with a 4th row of cable panel.
**2nd dec row** K6, k2 tog, k1(2:2), ★ work across patt panel, k1(2:2), skpo, k4, k2 tog, k1(2:2); rep from ★ once more.
Change to US 2 (2¾mm) needles.
Cont in patt until front measures 10¼in/26cm from cast on edge, ending with a 4th row of cable panel.
Change to US 3 (3¼mm) needles.
**1st inc row** K6, m1, k2(3:3), ★ work across patt panel, k2(3:3), m1, k4, m1, k2(3:3); rep from ★ to once more.
Cont in patt until front measures 12½in/32cm from cast on edge, ending with a 4th row of cable panel.
**2nd inc row** K6, m1, k3(4:4), ★ work across 1st row of patt panel, k3(4:4), m1, k4, m1, k3(4:4); rep from ★ once more. 80(85:89) sts.
Cont in patt until front measures 15(15¼:15¾)in/38(39:40)cm from cast on edge, ending with a 5th row of cable panel.

**Shape armhole and front neck**
Bind off 5 sts at beg of next row.
**1st row** K2, patt 4, skpo, patt to last 2 sts, k2 tog.
**2nd row** Patt to end.
**3rd row** K2, patt to last 2 sts, k2 tog.
**4th row** Patt 1 row.
Rep the last 4 rows 2(3:3) times more, then the first row again.
Keeping armhole edge straight cont to dec at neck edge on every 4th row until 46(48:51) sts rem.
Work straight until front matches Back to shoulders, ending at armhole edge.

**Shape shoulder**
Bind off 15(16:17) sts at beg of next and foll alt row.
Patt 1 row.
Bind off rem 16(16:17) sts.

**SLEEVES**
Using US 3 (3¼mm) needles cast on 58(60:64) sts.
**1st row** Work across 1st row of patt panel, k12(14:14), work across 1st row of patt panel.
**2nd row** Work across 2nd row of patt panel, k4(5:5), p4, k4(5:5), work across 2nd row of patt panel.
**3rd row** Work across 3rd row of patt panel, k4(5:5), C4F, k4(5:5), work across 3rd row of patt panel.
**4th row** Work across 4th row of patt panel, k4(5:5), p4, k4(5:5), work across 4th row of patt panel.
These 4 rows set the position for patt panels and form garter st and cable panels.
Cont in patt as set **at the same time** inc one st at each end of the 11th and every foll 6th row until there are 106(108:112) sts, working first 4(5:5) sts in garter st the next

**LOWER BACK EDGING**
With right side facing and US 2 (2¾mm)
needles pick up and k130(138:146) sts along
cast on edge.
Work as given for Sleeve Edging.

**NECK EDGING**
Join shoulder seams.
With right side facing and US 2 (2¾mm)
needles, pick up and k35 sts up right front
neck, 36 sts round back neck, 35 sts down left
front neck. 106 sts.
Work as given for Sleeve Edging.

**FINISH**
Sew in sleeves. Join side and sleeve seams. Sew
on buttons.

4 in cable panel, the rem sts in garter st.
Cont straight until sleeve measures 17(17¼:17¾)in/
43(44:45)cm from cast on edge, ending with a wrong
side row.

**Shape sleeve top**
Bind off 5 sts at beg of next 2 rows.
Dec one st at each end of next and 6(8:8) foll alt rows.
82(80:84) sts.
Work 1 row.
Bind off.

**SLEEVE EDGING**
With right side facing and US 2 (2¾mm) needles pick up
and k54(58:62) sts along cast on edge.
K 1 row.
**Bind off row (right side)** Bind off knitwise one st, [slip st
used in binding off back onto left hand needle, cast on 2 sts
knitwise, bind off 6 sts knitwise] to end. Fasten off.

**LOWER FRONT EDGING**
With right side facing and US 2 (2¾mm) needles pick up
and k70(74:78) sts along cast on edge.
Work as given for Sleeve Edging.

# SCANDINAVIAN jacket

A generous, zipped jacket based on the classic Scandinavian knitwear designs of bold black and white patterning with a hint of color. The Fair Isle and intarsia techniques used here are for the more experienced knitter.

## Materials

6(7) 50g balls of Debbie Bliss cotton double knitting in Main Color (M). Three balls of Black and two balls each of Blue and Red. Pair each of US 3 (3¼mm) and US 6 (4mm) knitting needles. 16(18)in/40(45)cm open-ended zip.

## Measurements

| To fit ages | 5-6 | 7-8 | years. |
|---|---|---|---|
| *Actual measurements* | | | |
| Chest | 35 | 38 | in |
| | 89 | 97 | cm |
| Length to shoulder | 19 | 21¼ | in |
| | 48 | 54 | cm |
| Sleeve length | 11¾ | 13¾ | in |
| | 30 | 35 | cm |

## Gauge

21 sts and 26 rows to 4in/10cm square over patt using US 6 (4mm) needles.

## Abbreviations

See page 127.

## Note

Read chart from right to left on right side rows and from left to right on wrong side rows (see page 113).
When working in patt, strand yarn not in use loosely across wrong side of work (see page 114).
When working motifs, use separate balls of yarn for each area of color and twist yarns together on wrong side to avoid holes (see page 116).

## BACK

With US 3 (3¼mm) needles and Red cast on 94(102) sts.
**1st rib row** K2, ★ p2, k2; rep from ★ to end.
Cont in M only.
**2nd rib row** P2, ★ k2, p2; rep from ★ to end.
Rep the last 2 rows 6(7) times more, inc 2 sts evenly across last row. 96(104) sts.
Change to US 6 (4mm) needles.
Beg with a k row cont in st st.
Work 2(4) rows.
Work in patt from Chart to end of row 80.
Rep from row 50 until back measures 19(21¼)in/48(54)cm from cast on edge, ending with a p row.

### Shape Shoulders

Bind off 11(12) sts at beg of next 4 rows and 10(11) sts at beg of foll 2 rows.
Bind off rem 32(34) sts.

## LEFT FRONT

With US 3 (3¼mm) needles and Red cast on 48(52)sts.
**1st rib row** K2, ★ p2, k2; rep from ★ to last 6 sts, p2, k4.
Working 2 sts at front edge in Red and garter st, and twisting yarns tog at back of work to avoid a hole, cont as folls:
**2nd rib row** K2 in Red, using M, p2, ★ k2, p2; rep from ★ to end.
**3rd rib row** Using M, k2, ★ p2, k2; rep from ★ to last 2 sts, k2 in Red.
**4th rib row** K2 in Red, using M, p2, ★ k2,

p2; rep from ★ to end.
Rep the last 2 rows 5(6) times more.
Change to US 6 (4mm) needles.
**Next row** Using M, k to last 2 sts, k2 in Red.
**Next row** K2 in Red, using M, p to end.
Rep the last 2 rows 0(1) times more.
Work in patt from Chart to match Back as folls:
**1st row** Work across 1st row of Chart, k2 in Red.
**2nd row** K2 in Red, work across 2nd row of Chart.
Cont in patt until work measures 17(19)in/43(48)cm from cast on edge, ending with a wrong side row.

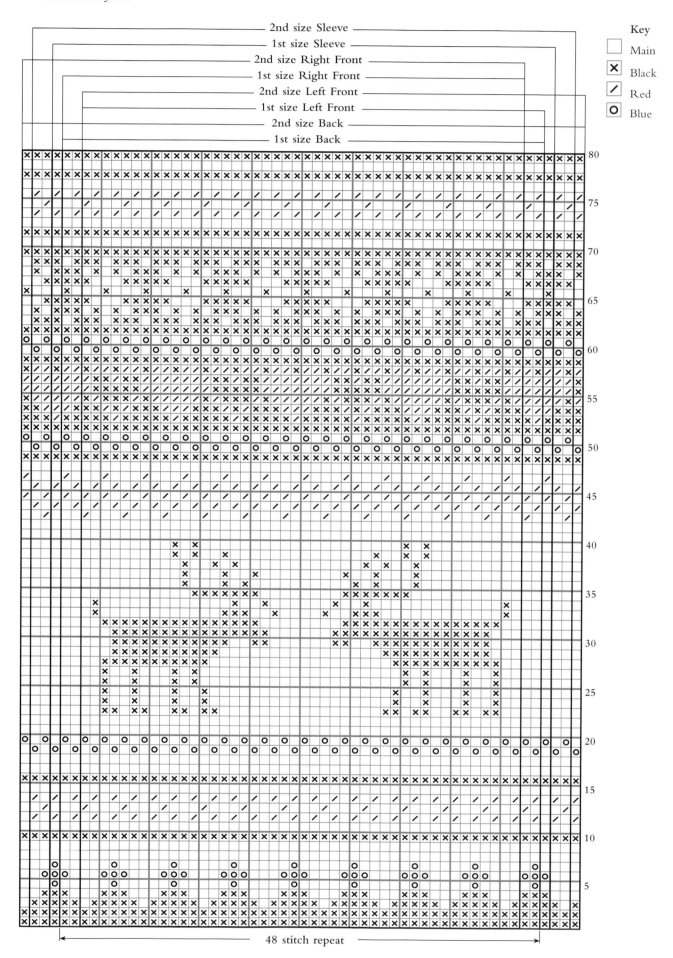

## Shape neck

**Next row** Patt to last 6(8) sts, leave these sts on a safety pin.
Dec one st at neck edge on every row until 32(35) sts rem.
Cont straight until front matches Back to shoulder shaping, ending at side edge.

## Shape shoulder

Bind off 11(12) sts at beg of next and foll alt row.
Work 1 row.
Bind off rem 10(11) sts.

## RIGHT FRONT

With US 3 (3¼mm) needles and Red cast on 48(52) sts.
**1st rib row** K4, ★ p2, k2; rep from ★ to end.
Working 2 sts at front edge in Red and garter st, and twisting yarns tog at back of work to avoid a hole, cont as folls:
**2nd rib row** Using M, p2, ★ k2, p2; rep from ★ to last 2 sts, k2 in Red.
**3rd rib row** K2 in Red, using M, k2, ★ p2, k2; rep from ★ to end.
**4th rib row** Using M, p2, ★ k2, p2; rep from ★ to last 2 sts, k2 in Red.
Rep the last 2 rows 5(6) times more.
Change to US 6 (4mm) needles.
**Next row** K2 in Red, using M, k to end.
**Next row** Using M, p to last 2 sts, k2 in Red.
Rep the last 2 rows 0(1) times more.
Complete to match Left Front.

## SLEEVES

With US 3 (3¼mm) needles and Red cast on 46(50) sts.
**1st rib row** K2, ★ p2, k2; rep from ★ to end.
Cont in M only.
**2nd rib row** P2, ★ k2, p2; rep from ★ to end.
Rep the last 2 rows 6(7) times more, inc 4 sts evenly across last row. 50(54) sts.
Change to US 6 (4mm) needles.
Beg with a k row cont in st st.
Work 2(4) rows.
Work in patt from Chart, **at the same time** inc one st at each end of next row, then on every 3rd and 4th row alternately until there are 84(94) sts.
Cont straight until sleeve measures 11¾(13¾)in/30(35)cm from cast on edge, ending with a wrong side row.
Bind off.

## COLLAR

Join shoulder seams.
With US 3 (3¼mm) needles right sides facing and Black, slip 6(8) sts from holder onto a needle, pick up and k15(16) sts up right front neck, 32(34) sts from back neck, 15(16) sts down left front neck, k6(8) sts from holder. 74(82) sts.
**1st row (right side)** K4, ★ p2, k2; rep from ★ to last 6 sts, p2, k4.
**2nd row** K2, ★ p2, k2; rep from ★ to end.
These 2 rows set the rib patt with garter st border.
**Next 2 rows** Rib to last 18 sts, turn.
**Next 2 rows** Rib to last 14 sts, turn.
**Next 2 rows** Rib to last 10 sts, turn.
**Next 2 rows** Rib to last 8 sts, turn.
Rib to end.
Work a further 2¾(3¼)in/7(8)cm in rib patt, ending with a wrong side row.
Change to Blue.
Rib 1 row.
Bind off.

## FINISH

With center of sleeves to shoulder seam, sew on sleeves. Join side and sleeve seams. Sew in zip.

# COTTON/SILK aran

Combining cables with seed stitch, this design also has gently rolling hems. The shorter length and raglan shaping gives a flattering, body-contouring effect. Knitted in my cotton with silk, this is a sweater for more special occasions, too.

## PANEL A

(worked over 15 sts)

1st row (right side) P5, T5L, p5.
2nd row K5, p2, k1, p2, k5.
3rd row P4, T3B, k1, T3F, p4.
4th row K4, p2, k1, p1, k1, p2, k4.
5th row P3, T3B, k1, p1, k1, T3F, p3.
6th row K3, p2, [k1, p1] twice, k1, p2, k3.
7th row P2, T3B, [k1, p1] twice, k1, T3F, p2.
8th row K2, p2, [k1, p1] 3 times, k1, p2, k2.
9th row P1, T3B, [k1, p1] 3 times, k1, T3F, p1.
10th row K1, p2, [k1, p1] 4 times, k1, p2, k1.
11th row P1, k3, [p1, k1] 3 times, k4, p1.
12th row K1, p2, [k1, p1] 4 times, k1, p2, k1.
13th row P1, T3F, [k1, p1] 3 times, k1, T3B, p1.
14th row As 8th row.
15th row P2, T3F, [k1, p1] twice, k1, T3B, p2.
16th row As 6th row.
17th row P3, T3F, k1, p1, k1, T3B, p3.
18th row As 4th row.
19th row P4, T3F, k1, T3B, p4.
20th row As 2nd row.
21st row P5, T5L, p5.
22nd row As 2nd row.
23rd row P4, T3B, p1, T3F, p4.
24th row K4, p2, k3, p2, k4.
25th row P4, k2, p3, k2, p4.
26th row K4, p2, k3, p2, k4.
27th row P4, T3F, p1, T3B, p4.
28th row As 2nd row.
These 28 rows form the patt and are repeated throughout.

## Materials

20(21) 50g balls of Debbie Bliss cotton/silk aran. Pair each of US 5 (3¾mm), US 6 (4mm) and US 7 (4½mm) knitting needles. Cable needle.

## Measurements

| To fit bust | 32-34 | 36-38 | in |
|---|---|---|---|
| | 82-87 | 92-97 | cm |

*Actual measurements*

| Bust | 38 | 41¾ | in |
|---|---|---|---|
| | 96 | 106 | cm |
| Length to shoulder | 19¼ | 20½ | in |
| | 49 | 52 | cm |
| Sleeve length | 18 | 18 | in |
| | 46 | 46 | cm |

## Gauge

18 sts and 24 rows to 4in/10cm square over st st using US 7 (4½mm) needles.

## Abbreviations

**T3F** – slip next 2 sts on cable needle and hold at front of work, p1, then k2 from cable needle.
**T3B** – slip next st on cable needle and hold at back of work, k2, then p1 from cable needle.
**T5L** – slip next 2 sts on cable needle and hold at front of work, k2, p1, then k2 from cable needle.
**C4F** – cable 4 front, slip next 2 sts on cable needle and hold at front of work, k2, then k2 from cable needle.
**C4B** – cable 4 back, slip next 2 sts on cable needle and hold at back of work, k2, then k2 from cable needle.
See also page 127.

## PANEL B

(worked over 17 sts)

**1st row (right side)** P6, T5L, p6.

**2nd row** K6, p2, k1, p2, k6.

**3rd row** P5, T3B, k1, T3F, p5.

**4th row** K5, p2, k1, p1, k1, p2, k5.

**5th row** P4, T3B, k1, p1, k1, T3F, p4.

**6th row** K4, p2, [k1, p1] twice, k1, p2, k4.

**7th row** P3, T3B, [k1, p1] twice, k1, T3F, p3.

**8th row** K3, p2, [k1, p1] 3 times, k1, p2, k3.

**9th row** P2, T3B, [k1, p1] 3 times, k1, T3F, p2.

**10th row** K2, p2, [k1, p1] 4 times, k1, p2, k2.

**11th row** P1, T3B, [k1, p1] 4 times, k1, T3F, p1.

**12th row** K1, p2, [k1, p1] 5 times, k1, p2, k1.

These 12 rows form the patt and are repeated throughout.

## BACK AND FRONT

With US 6 (4mm) needles cast on 85(95) sts.

Starting with a k row, work 5 rows st st.

**Inc row** P5, [m1, p5] 16(18) times. 101(113) sts.

Change to US 7 (4½mm) needles.

Cont in patt.

**1st row** [K1, p1] 2(5) times, p1, k4, work across 1st row of panel A, k4, p1, k8, p1, k4, work across 1st row of panel B, k4, p1, k8, p1, k4, work across 1st row of panel A, k4, p1, [p1, k1] 2(5) times.

**2nd row** [P1, k1] 2(5) times, k1, p4, work across 2nd row of panel A, p4, k1, p8, k1, p4, work across 2nd row of panel B, p4, k1, p8, k1, p4, work across 2nd row of panel A, p4, k1, [k1, p1] 2(5) times.

**3rd row** [P1, k1] 2(5) times, p1, C4F, work across 3rd row of panel A, C4F, p1, C4B, C4F, p1, C4F, work across 3rd row of panel B, C4B, p1, C4B, C4F, p1, C4B, work across 3rd row of panel A, C4B, p1, [k1, p1] 2(5) times.

**4th row** [K1, p1] 2(5) times, k1, p4, work across 4th row of panel A, p4, k1, p8, k1, p4, work across 4th row of panel B, p4, k1, p8, k1, p4, work across 4th row of panel A, p4, k1, [p1, k1] 2(5) times.

These 4 rows set the patt.

Cont in patt until back measures 12½in/32cm from cast on edge, ending 12th row of panel B.

### Shape raglans

Bind off 10(13) sts at beg of next 2 rows.

**Next row** K2, skpo, patt to last 4 sts, k2 tog, k2.

**Next row** P3, patt to last 3 sts, p3.

Rep the last 2 rows until 35 sts rem, ending with a right side row.

**Next row** P2 tog, patt to last 2 sts, p2 tog. 33 sts.

Leave rem sts on a holder.

## SLEEVES

With US 6 (4mm) needles cast on 45 sts.

Starting with a k row, work 5 rows st st.

**Inc row** P5, [m1, p5] 8 times. 53 sts.

Change to US 7 (4½mm) needles.

Cont in patt.

**1st row** K4, p1, k8, p1, k4, work across 1st row of panel B, k4, p1, k8, p1, k4.

**2nd row** P4, k1, p8, k1, p4, work across 2nd row of panel B, p4, k1, p8, k1, p4.

**3rd row** C4F, p1, C4B, C4F, p1, C4F, work across 3rd row of panel B, C4B, p1, C4B, C4F, p1, C4B.

**4th row** P4, k1, p8, k1, p4, work across 4th row of panel B, p4, k1, p8, k1, p4.

These 4 rows set the patt.

Keeping continuity of patt, inc one st at each end of the next and every foll 6th(5th) row until there are 87(93) sts, working extra sts into patt as folls: first st into "p1" rib and rem 16(19) sts into double seed st.

Cont straight until sleeve measures 19(19)in/48(48)cm from cast on edge, ending with a wrong side row.

### Shape raglans

Bind off 10(13) sts at beg of next 2 rows.

*2nd size only*

**Next row** K2, skpo, patt to last 4 sts, k2 tog, k2.

**Next row** P3, patt to last 3 sts, p3.

**Next row** K3, patt to last 3 sts, k3.

**Next row** P3, patt to last 3 sts, p3.

Rep the last 4 rows twice more.

*Both sizes*

**Next row** K2, skpo, patt to last 4 sts, k2 tog, k2.

**Next row** P3, patt to last 3 sts, p3.

Rep the last 2 rows until 21 sts rem, ending with a right side row.

**Next row** P2 tog, patt to last 2 sts, p2 tog. 19 sts.

Leave rem sts on a holder.

**NECKBAND**

Join both front and right back raglan seams.
With US 5 (3¾mm) needles, right side facing,
work as folls: [k1, p1] 11 times, p1, patt 4, [p1,
k1] 8 times, p1, patt 4, p2, k1, [p1, k1] 11
times, p2, patt 4, [p1, k1] 8 times, p1, patt 4,
p2, k1, p1. 104 sts.
Work a further 10 rows in patt as set, dec 2 sts
over each cable on last row.
96 sts
Beg with a k row, work 4 rows in st st.
Bind off.

**FINISH**

Join left back raglan and neckband seams
reversing last 4 rows of seam. Join side and
sleeve seams.

# SIMPLE JACKET hat and bootees

Ideal for the relatively inexperienced knitter, this simple garter stitch jacket has cuffs edged in a contrasting color, plus matching bootees and a hat. There is also an accompanying throw on page 70.

## Materials

Jacket: 7(8:9) 50g balls of Debbie Bliss cotton double knitting in Main Color (M). One ball in Contrast Color (C). Pair each of US 5 (3¾mm) and US 6 (4mm) knitting needles. 6(7:7) buttons.
Bootees: One 50g ball of Debbie Bliss cotton double knitting in each of Main Color (M) and Contrast Color (C). Pair US 3 (3¼mm) knitting needles.
Hat: One 50g ball of Debbie Bliss cotton double knitting in each of Main Color (M) and Contrast Color (C). Pair US 6 (4mm) knitting needles.

## Measurements

**Jacket**

| To fit age | 6-9 | 9-12 | 12-24 | months. |
|---|---|---|---|---|
| *Actual measurements* | | | | |
| Chest | 22 | 24½ | 27½ | in |
| | 56 | 62 | 70 | cm |
| Length to shoulder | 10¼ | 11¾ | 13½ | in |
| | 26 | 30 | 34 | cm |
| Sleeve length | | | | |
| (cuff turned back) | 6¼ | 7 | 8 | in |
| | 16 | 18 | 20 | cm |
| **Hat** | | | | |
| To fit age | 6-9 | 9-12 | 12-24 | months. |
| **Bootees** | | | | |
| To fit age | 6-12 | months. | | |

## Gauge

20 sts and 40 rows to 4in/10cm square over garter st (every row k) using US 6 (4mm) needles.

## Abbreviations

See page 127.

## JACKET

### POCKET LININGS (MAKE 2)

With US 6 (4mm) needles and M cast on 15(17:19) sts.
K 24(28:32) rows. Leave these sts on a holder.

### BACK AND FRONTS

With US 6 (4mm) needles and C cast on 112(124:140) sts.
K 1 row.
Cont in M.
K 24(28:32) rows.

## Place pockets

**Next row** K6(7:8), bind off 15(17:19) sts, k next 69(75:85) sts, bind off 15(17:19) sts, k to end.

**Next row** K6(7:8), k across sts of first pocket lining, k70(76:86) sts, k across sts of second pocket lining, k6(7:8).

Cont in straight in garter st until work measures 6(6¾:7½)in/15(17:19)cm from cast on edge, ending with a wrong side row.

## Divide for back and fronts

**Next row** K28(31:35), leave these sts on a holder for right front, k next 56(62:70), leave these sts on a holder for back, k to end.

## LEFT FRONT

Work straight on last set of 28(31:35) sts until front measures 8¾(9¾:11)in/22(25:28)cm from cast on edge, ending at neck edge.

## Shape neck

**Next row** K6(7:8) sts, leave these sts on a safety pin, k to end.

Dec one st at neck edge on every row until 14(16:18) sts rem.

Work straight until front measures

10¼(11¾:13½)in/26(30:34)cm from cast on edge, ending at armhole edge.

## Shape shoulder

Bind off.

## BACK

With wrong side facing, rejoin yarn to next st.

Work straight until back measures same as Left Front to shoulder, ending with a wrong side row.

## Shape shoulders

Bind off 14(16:18) sts at beg of next 2 rows.

Leave rem 28(30:34) sts on a spare needle.

## RIGHT FRONT

With wrong side facing, rejoin yarn to next st, work to match Left Front, reversing all shapings.

## SLEEVES

With US 6 (4mm) needles and C cast on 32(34:38) sts.

K 1 row.

Cont in M.

K 16 rows.

Change to US 5 (3¾mm) needles.

K 16 rows.

Change to US 6 (4mm) needles

Cont in garter st, inc one st at each end of the next and every foll 5th row until there are 48(56:64) sts.

Cont straight until sleeve measures 8(8½:9½)in/20(22:24)cm from cast on edge, ending with a wrong side row.

Bind off.

## NECKBAND

Join shoulder seams.

With right side facing, using US 5 (3¾mm) needles and C, k6(7:8) sts from safety pin, pick up and k12(14:16) sts up right front neck edge, k across 28(30:34) sts on back neck, pick up and k12(14:16) sts down left side of front neck, k6(7:8) sts from safety pin. 64(72:82) sts.

K 2 rows.

Bind off.

## BUTTONBAND

With right side facing, using US 5 (3¾mm) needles and C, pick up and k46(52:58) sts along left front edge.

K 2 rows.

Bind off.

## BUTTONHOLE BAND

With right side facing, using US 5 (3¾mm) needles and C, pick up and k46(52:58) sts along right front edge.

**Buttonhole row** K2(1:1) sts, [k2 tog, yf, k6(6:7) sts] 5(6:6) times, k2 tog, yf, k2(1:1).

K 1 row.

Bind off.

## FINISH

Join sleeve seams, reversing seam on cuff for 1¾in/4cm. Sew in sleeves. Sew on buttons.

## BOOTEES

With US 3 (3¾mm) needles and M, cast on 48 sts.

K 1 row.

**1st row** K1, yf, k22, yf, k2, yf, k22, yf, k1.

**2nd and 4 foll alt rows** K to end, working k1b into yf of previous row.

**3rd row** K2, yf, k23, yf, k2, yf, k23, yf, k2.

**5th row** K3, yf, k24, yf, k2, yf, k24, yf, k3. 60 sts.

**6th row** K to end, working k1b into yf of previous row.

K 6 rows.

### Shape top

**Next row** K26, k3 tog, k2, k3 togb, k26.

K 1 row.

**Next row** K24, k3 tog, k2, k3 togb, k24.

K 1 row.

**Next row** K22, k3 tog, k2, k3 togb, k22.

K 1 row.

**Next row** K20, k3 tog, k2, k3 togb, k20.

K 1 row.

**Next row** K18, k3 tog, k2, k3 togb, k18.

K 1 row. 40 sts.

**Next row** K17, k2 tog, k2, skpo, k17.

K 1 row.

**FINISH**
Join seam, reversing seam on last 4 rows. Using C, make pom-poms and sew to toes.

**HAT**
With US 6 (4mm) needles and C, cast on 71(81:91) sts.
Starting with a k row work 6 rows st st.
Cont in M.
Cont in garter st.
Work 36 rows.
**1st dec row** K1, [k2 tog, k8] 7(8:9) times.
K 1 row.
**2nd dec row** K1, [k2 tog, k7] 7(8:9) times.
K 1 row.
**3rd dec row** K1, [k2 tog, k6] 7(8:9) times.
K 1 row.
Cont to dec in this way until 15(17:19) sts rem.
**Next row** K1, [k2 tog] to end. 8(9:10) sts.
Break off yarn thread through rem sts, pull up and secure.
Join seam. Using C, make a pom-pom and sew to crown.

**Next row** K16, k2 tog, k2, skpo, k16.
K 1 row.
Cont in this way dec 2 sts on every alt row until 30 sts rem.
K 7 rows.
**Next row** K15, turn and k 4 rows.
Cont in C.
K 1 row.
Bind off.
With right side facing, rejoin M to rem sts, k to end.
K 4 rows.
Cont in C.
K 1 row.
Bind off.

# TECHNIQUES

In this section you will find illustrations and explanations of the more complex techniques, such as color and cable knitting, used in some of the patterns in this book.

Always read the instructions given on the knitting pattern as well as referring to the specific technique illustrated in this section, as there may be additional elements to be aware of.

## WORKING FROM A CHART

Color designs are usually illustrated with symbols or colors on a graph. Each square represents one stitch and one row. In the same way that you knit upwards from the bottom of your work, so you read the chart from the bottom row upwards.

In a repeated design the chart will show how many stitches are repeated across the row and there may be edge stitches either side of this repeat. The edge stitches are worked once at the beginning and end of the row and the repeat is worked as many times as necessary.

Unless otherwise stated, the first row of the chart is the first row of the color pattern and is usually a knit row, which is followed by reading the chart from right to left. The second row is usually a purl row and for this the chart is read from left to right.

Individual motifs, such as the flower shown below, do not always start on a right side row, depending on where they are placed on the garment. If they start on a wrong side row, the first row of the chart is read from left to right.

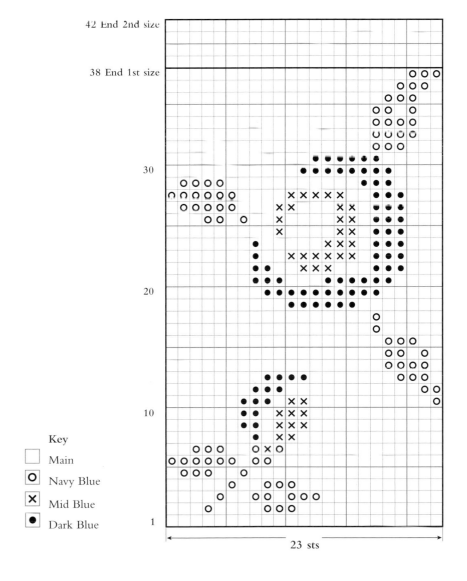

**Key**
- Main
- Navy Blue
- Mid Blue
- Dark Blue

42 End 2nd size
38 End 1st size
30
20
10
1

23 sts

# FAIR ISLE KNITTING

Stranding is used when the yarn not being used is left at the back of the work until needed. The loops formed by stranding are called "floats" and it is important to ensure that they are not pulled too tightly when working the next stitch, as this will pull in your knitting. If the gap between the colors is more than four stitches the weaving in method is preferable, as this prevents floats becoming too long and stopping the fabric having the right amount of elasticity. Many color patterns will use both techniques and you should choose the one that is the most appropriate to a particular part of the design.

## STRANDING

**1** On a knit row, hold the first color in your right hand and the second color in your left hand. Knit the required number of stitches as usual with the first color, carrying the second color loosely across the wrong side of the work.

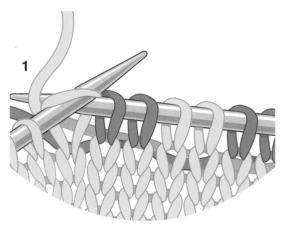

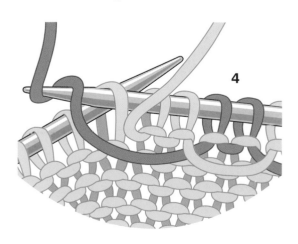

**2** To knit a stitch in the second color, insert the right hand needle into the next stitch then draw a loop through from the yarn held in the left hand, carrying the yarn in the right hand loosely across the wrong side until required.

**3** On a purl row, hold the yarns as for the knit rows. Purl the required number of stitches as usual with the first color, carrying the second color loosely across these stitches on the wrong side of the work.

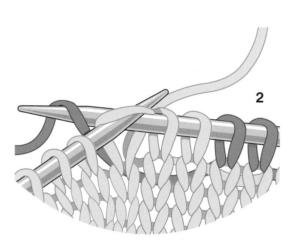

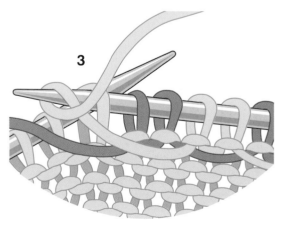

**4** To purl a stitch in the second color, insert the right hand needle into the next stitch then draw a loop through from the yarn held in the left hand, carrying the yarn in the right hand loosely across the wrong side until next required.

# WEAVING

In weaving in, or knitting in, the floats are caught in by the working yarn on every third or fourth stitch. Weaving in on alternate stitches can distort stitches and alter the gauge.

**1** Insert the right hand needle into the stitch. Lay the contrast yarn over the point of the right hand needle then knit the stitch in the usual way, taking care not to knit in the contrast yarn.

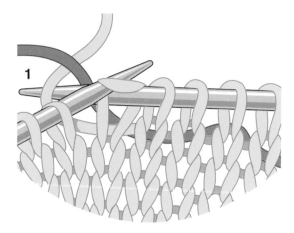

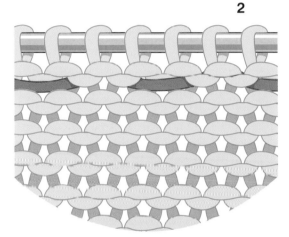

**2** When you knit the next stitch, the contrast yarn will have been caught in. Use the same method to catch in the yarn on the purl rows.

*A simple Fair Isle border on a seed stitch scarf.*

*The back of stranded and woven fabric can look very neat if the technique is worked carefully.*

# INTARSIA KNITTING

Intarsia is the name given to color knitting where the pattern is worked in large blocks of color at a time, requiring a separate length or ball of yarn for each area of color, as the yarn must not be stranded at the back.

## DIAGONAL COLOR CHANGE WITH A SLANT TO THE LEFT

**1** This illustration shows a color change on the wrong side of the work.

Use separate lengths or balls of yarn for each block of color. On a right side row, with the yarns at the back of the work, the crossing of colors at joins happens automatically because of the encroaching nature of the pattern. On a wrong side row, with the yarns at the front of the work, take the first color over the second color, drop it then pick up the second color underneath the first color thus crossing the two colors together.

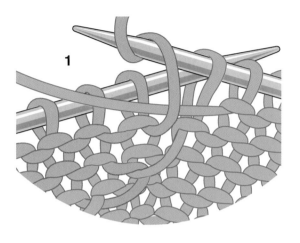

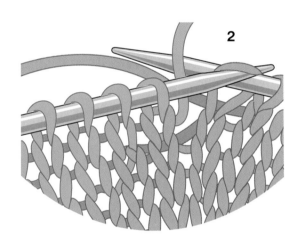

## VERTICAL COLOR CHANGE

**3** This illustration shows a color change on the wrong side of the work.

Use separate lengths or balls of yarn for each block of color. Work in the first color to the color change, then drop the first color, pick up the second color underneath the first color, crossing the two colors over before working the next stitch in the second color. The first stitch after a color change is worked firmly to avoid a gap forming between colors. This technique ensures that the yarns are crossed on every row and gives a neat vertical line between colors on the right side, and a vertical line of loops in each color on the wrong side.

## DIAGONAL COLOR CHANGE WITH A SLANT TO THE RIGHT

**2** This illustration shows a color change on the right side of the work.

Use separate lengths or balls of yarn for each block of color. On a right side row, with the yarns at the back of the work, take the first color over the second color, drop it then pick up the second color underneath the first color thus crossing the two colors over. On a wrong side row, with the yarns at the front of the work, the crossing of the two colors at the joins happens automatically because of the encroaching nature of the pattern.

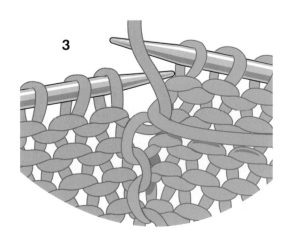

Intarsia is the perfect technique for knitting separated
motifs worked across the knitted fabric.

A good design touch is to use the same colors
for motifs and borders on a garment.

When working larger intarsia motifs do
not cut the lengths of yarn too short.

# BASIC CABLE

Cables are made by crossing one group of stitches over another. The number of stitches that are crossed can vary to make larger and smaller cables, and the number of rows between each crossover can also vary. Once the basic cable technique has been mastered, it can be used to reproduce many pattern variations. The cable shown here is a basic four-stitch pattern in stockinette stitch, worked on a reverse stockinette stitch background. Where different cables are given in the patterns, use the same basic technique, but follow the instructions given with the pattern.

## CABLE 4 FRONT (C4F)

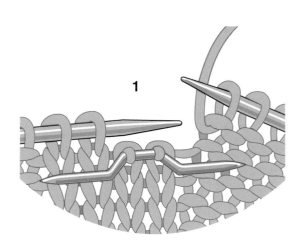

**1** On a right side row, work to the position of the cable panel then slip the next two stitches onto the cable needle, leaving it at the front of the work.

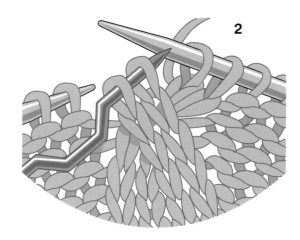

**2** Working behind the cable needle, knit the next two stitches from the left hand needle.

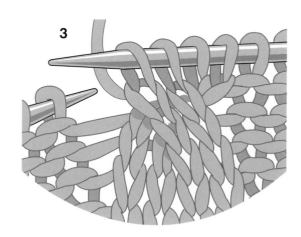

**3** Now knit the two stitches from the cable needle to produce a cable that crosses to the left.
For a cable 4 back (C4B) leave the stitches on the cable needle at the back of the work.

Cables work well combined with bobbles
to give more intricate patterns.

An all-over cable pattern can be used
as a center panel for a garment.

Classic diamond cables give a twist to
a contemporary knitwear design.

# KNITTING WITH BEADS

Beads can be sewn onto your finished knitting or knitted in. When knitted in the beads "hang" very slightly on the surface of the fabric from the strand of yarn at the front of the slipped stitch.

Most patterns specify the number of beads to be threaded on to each ball of yarn. If not, thread up one ball with more beads than you will need, then count the number used after completing that ball. It is important to thread on the correct number of beads (or more) before beginning to knit; once the ball is started you will not be able to add more unless you unwind the ball and add them from the other end, or break the yarn.

The knitted fabric should be fairly firm or the beads may slip through to the wrong side, and the additional weight of the beads may drag a loosely knitted garment out of shape. The beads should be a suitable weight for the yarn and must have a large enough hole for double-thickness yarn to pass through.

**1** If the yarn and needle are thin enough you can thread them straight through the beads. If not, use the method shown here.

Fold a length of sewing cotton in half and thread both ends through a sewing needle. Thread the end of the yarn through the loop in the sewing cotton and fold it back on itself. Thread beads along the needle, down the sewing cotton and onto the yarn until you have the number of beads on the yarn that your pattern requires.

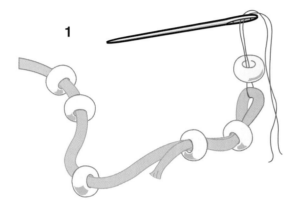

**2** On a right side row, knit to the position of the beaded stitch. Bring the yarn forward to the front of the work and push a bead down the yarn close to the last stitch so that it lies over the front of the next stitch.

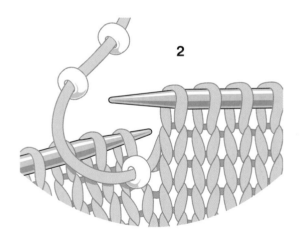

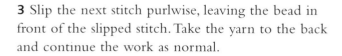

**3** Slip the next stitch purlwise, leaving the bead in front of the slipped stitch. Take the yarn to the back and continue the work as normal.

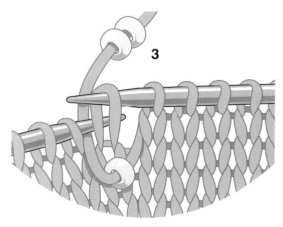

*Beads can be knitted in randomly
or in a more structured design.*

*A beaded edge can be created by knitting in
beads on the cast on and bound off edges.*

# EMBROIDERY

Knitted fabric is a good base for simple embroidery, as you can use the horizontal and vertical lines as guides in placing the stitches. Choose your embroidery thread or yarn carefully; if it is too thin it can disappear into the knitted fabric, and if it is too thick it can distort the fabric. Before you start stitching, fasten the end of the thread on the reverse of the fabric or leave a loose end to weave in later. To follow a specific embroidery pattern, you can trace the design onto tissue paper and pin this in place on the knitted fabric. Embroider through the paper and fabric and then pull away the paper. The following stitches are ones that I like to use and those that are worked on the Embroidered Dress on page 8.

## FRENCH KNOTS

Bring the needle and thread up through the knitted fabric and then wind the thread twice around the needle. Keeping the thread taut around the needle, take the needle back down through the fabric very close to where it first emerged. Bring the needle up again in the right position for the next knot.

## LAZY DAISY

Bring the needle and thread up through the knitted fabric. Take it down through the fabric in the same place and bring the tip of it up through the fabric a short distance away. Loop the thread under the needle and then pull the needle right through. Take the needle down through the fabric over the loop to secure it in place. Bring the needle up again in the right position for the next lazy daisy stitch.

## SATIN STITCH

Work parallel stitches, close together, bringing the needle up and taking it down through the knitted fabric on the edges of the design. Do not pull the thread tightly or you will distort the fabric.

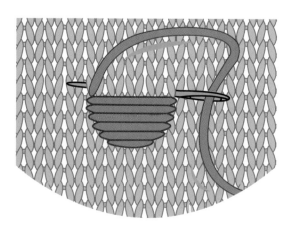

*The diagram above shows where to place the embroidery stitches to create the floral swag shown at the top (see also page 8).*

# FINISH

Sloppy sewing up can ruin a beautifully knitted garment, but by using the methods shown here you can create virtually invisible seams. Check the yarn ball band to see if there are any special pressing instructions you must follow before you start sewing.

## JOINING A SIDE SEAM ON STOCKINETTE STITCH FABRIC (MATTRESS STITCH)

Right sides up, lay the pieces to be joined flat and edge to edge. Thread a blunt-pointed needle with yarn and attach the yarn to the back of one side. Bring the needle out to the front between the edge stitch and the second stitch in the first row. Insert the needle between the edge stitch and the second stitch in the first row on the opposite side. Pass the needle under the loops of one or two rows, then bring it back through to the front. Insert the needle into the hole that the last stitch came out of on the first side and pass it under the loops of one or two rows to emerge in the same place as on the opposite side. Repeat this zigzag action, always taking the needle under the strands that correspond exactly to those on the other side, taking care not to miss any rows. After a few stitches pull up the yarn thus closing the seam. Make sure that the seam is at the same gauge as the rest of the fabric.

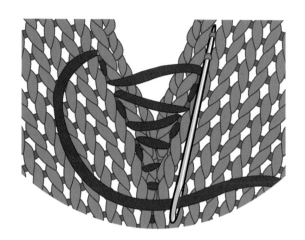

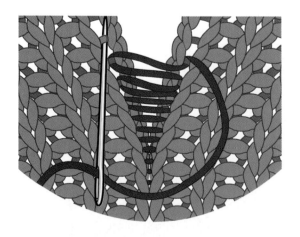

## JOINING A SIDE SEAM ON SINGLE RIB

When joining two ribbed sections together, it is best to take in only half a stitch on either side, so that when the two pieces are drawn together one complete knit stitch in formed along the seam. Join the seam in the same way as for stockinette stitch but pass the needle under the loop of one row at a time rather than two. To join double rib, use the same method, but take in a whole stitch, as with mattress stitch, for the least visible seam.

## JOINING TWO BOUND OFF EDGES

**1** Two bound off edges can be joined together in a similar way as for a side seam. Bring the needle out in the center of the first stitch below the bound off stitch on one side. Insert the needle in the center of the first stitch on the opposite side and bring it out in the center of the next stitch.

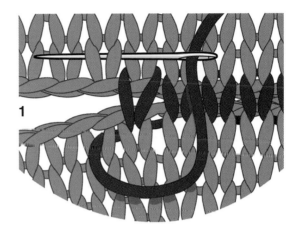

**2** Return to the first stitch and insert the needle in the center of the first stitch, bring it out in the center of the next stitch.

*Wonderfully neat, professional-looking seams can be achieved using proper joining stitches.*

# BASIC INFORMATION

## NOTES

In the patterns figures for larger sizes are given in round ( )brackets. Where only one size is given this means that it applies to all sizes.

Work the figures in the square [ ] brackets the number of times stated. Where 0 appears no stitches or rows are worked for this size.

The quantities of yarn stated are based on average requirements and are therefore approximate. A small variation in gauge can alter the amount of yarn you use so it is important to work a gauge square before you start your project.

My patterns quote the actual size of the finished garment rather than the bust/chest of the wearer and this will tell you how much ease the design has, whether it is close fitting or generously sized. Check these measurements before you knit; if want to finish the design with more or less ease you may have to knit up a larger or smaller size.

## YARNS

The following descriptions of the yarns used in this book are a guide to the yarn weight and type. Turn to page 128 for a list of international distributors.

**Debbie Bliss wool/cotton:** a 50% merino wool, 50% cotton lightweight yarn. Approximately107m/50g ball.

**Debbie Bliss cotton double knitting:** a 100% pure cotton double knitting yarn. Approximately 83m/50g ball.

**Debbie Bliss cotton/silk:** a 80% pure cotton, 20% silk aran weight yarn. Approximately 63m/50g ball.

Always try to buy the yarn quoted in the pattern, but if you do use a substitute, buy a yarn with the same metreage and wherever possible, the same fibre content. It is essential to compare the metreage as a ball of yarn that weighs the same may be a different length, so you may need to buy more or less yarn.

Also check dye lots. Buy the full amount of yarn quoted, checking that all the balls are from the same dye lot. If you buy yarn in small amounts you may find that the retailer has received a new dye lot and the color may be subtly different.

## GAUGE

Each pattern in the book specifies a gauge: the number of stitches and rows per centimetre or inch that should be obtained with the given needles, yarn and stitch pattern. However eager you are to start a pattern you should always make time to work a gauge square to avoid disappointment when you have finished the garment. Tighter or looser gauge can make the difference between a smaller or larger garment than the one you wanted and alter the yarn amounts you use.

To knit a gauge square, use the same yarn, needles, and stitch pattern as those quoted in the gauge note, which appears before the main part of the pattern. Knit a sample at least 5in/13cm square. Smooth out the finished sample on a flat surface, but make sure you do not stretch it. To check the stitch gauge, place a ruler horizontally on the sample and mark 4in/10cm with pins. To check the row gauge place the ruler vertically on the sample and mark 4in/10cm with pins. Count the number of stitches and rows between the pins.

If you have more stitches and rows than that quoted in the gauge note then your knitting is too tight and you need to try again using a larger needle. If you have less stitches and rows, your knitting is too loose and you need to try again using a smaller needle. As a lot of patterns quote the length in measurement rather than rows, it is more important that you achieve the correct stitch gauge.

The following terms may be unfamiliar to US readers

| UK terms | US terms |
|---|---|
| Aran wool | "fisherman yarn" |
| ball band | yarn wrapper |
| double knitting yarn | a yarn between worsted and sport |
| rib | ribbing |
| yarn forward | yarn over |
| yarn over needle | yarn over |
| yarn round needle | yarn over |

## ABBREVIATIONS

Some knitting terms may be unfamiliar to readers. The list below gives the general abbreviations that are used throughout the book. More specific abbreviations are explained at the beginning of the relevant pattern.

**alt** = alternate
**beg** = beginning
**cont** = continu(e)(ing)
**cm** = centimetre(s)
**dec** = decrease(ing)
**foll** = follow(s)(ing)
**g** = gram(mes)
**in** = inch(es)
**inc** = increase one stitch by working into the front and back of the next stitch
**k** = knit
**k1b** = knit through back of loop
**m1(p)** = make one by picking up the loop between the stitch just worked and the next stitch and knitting (purling) into the back of it.
**mm** = millimetre(s)
**patt** = pattern
**p** = purl
**p1b** = purl through back of loop
**psso** = pass slipped stitch over
**rem** = remain(ing)
**rep** = repeat(ing)
**skpo** = slip one, knit one, pass slipped stitch over
**sl** = slip
**st(s)** = stitch(es)
**st st** = stockinette stitch
**tog** = together
**togb** = together through back of loops
**yb** = yarn back
**yf** = yarn forward
**yon** = yarn over needle
**yrn** = yarn around needle

## CARE OF GARMENTS

Check the ball band for washing instructions. All the yarns used are machine washable on a delicate cycle, although personally I still prefer to handwash my handknits as much as possible. Dry them flat on a towel, patting them into shape. Do not dry them near direct heat such as a radiator. It is better to store your handknits loosely folded to let them "breathe".

# ACKNOWLEDGEMENTS

This book would not have been possible without the dedication of the following:

Most importantly, the knitters, who always work with impossible deadlines:
Dorothy Bayley, Cynthia Brent, Pat Church, Jaqui Dunt, Janet Fagan, Penny Hill, Shirley Kennet, Maisie Lawrence, Beryl Salter and Frances Wallace.

Jane Bunce, for her commitment to all my projects, and the butterfly cardigan and bag, and Jane Crowfoot, for the lovely embroidery, the tartan beaded bag, and her beautiful daughter, Summer.

Craig Fordham, the photographer, for the beautiful photography and Rob, his assistant, for his uncanny impersonations of owls and Toby Jugs.

Marilyn Wilson, the pattern checker, for her hard work and thorough checking.

Penny Hill, for pattern compiling.

Kate Haxell, the project manager, for her support and making it all work.

Sammi Bell, for the lovely styling.

Georgina Harris, managing editor, for her enthusiasm.

Cindy Richards and Mark Collins, for initiating the project.

Heather Jeeves, for being a terrific agent.

The models, for making the book such fun to work on: Aggie, Brandon, Caitlin, Ceri, Charlie, Harry, Julia, Lavinia, Michelle, Nou, Scarlet, Somerset, Summer and Tally.

# DISTRIBUTORS

Debbie Bliss yarns are available in knitting stores. Call your distributor for more details.

**UK AND EUROPE**
**Designer Yarns Ltd**
1 Tivoli Place
Ilkey
West Yorkshire LS29 8SU

Tel: 01943 604123
Fax: 01943 600320
Email: tivolipl@aol.com

**USA**
**Knitting Fever Inc**
35, Debevoise Avenue
Roosevelt
New York 11575

Tel: 516 546 3600
Fax: 516 546 6871
Email: www.knittingfever.com

**CANADA**
**Diamond Yarns Ltd**
155 Martin Ross Avenue
Unit 3
Toronto
Ontario M3J 2L9

Tel: 416 736 6111
Fax: 416 736 6112
Email: www.diamondyarn.com

**JAPAN**
**Eisaku Noro and Co Ltd**
55 Shimoda Ohibino Azaichou,
Ichinomita Aichi
491 0105

Tel: 52 203 5100
Fax: 52 203 5077

**AUSTRALIA**
**Sunspun Inspirations**
185 Canterbury Road
Canterbury
VIC 3126

Tel: 039 888 5658
Email: sunspun@labyrinth.net.au